I0831893

Mike Barry and the Kentucky Irish American

Racing Form

Mike Barry and the Kentucky Irish American

AN ANTHOLOGY

CLYDE F. CREWS
Editor

With a Foreword by
MRS. BARRY BINGHAM, SR.

THE UNIVERSITY PRESS OF KENTUCKY

Scholarly publisher for the Commonwealth,
serving Bellarmine College, Berea College, Centre
College of Kentucky, Eastern Kentucky University,
The Filson Club, Georgetown College, Kentucky
Historical Society, Kentucky State University,
Morehead State University, Murray State University,
Northern Kentucky University, Transylvania University,
University of Kentucky, University of Louisville,
and Western Kentucky University.

Editorial and Sales Offices: Lexington, Kentucky 40508-4008

Frontispiece: Mike Barry (1909-1992). Courtesy of Richard Northern.

Library of Congress Cataloging-in-Publication Data

Mike Barry and the Kentucky Irish American : an anthology / Clyde F. Crews, editor ; with a foreword by Mrs. Barry Bingham, Sr.
p. cm.
Includes bibliographical references and index.
ISBN 0-8131-1898-0 (acid-free paper)
1. Irish Americans—Kentucky—Louisville—Newspapers. 2. Barry, Mike, 1909–1992. 3. United States—Politics and government—1945–1989. 4. Kentucky—Politics and government—1951–
I. Crews, Clyde F. II. Kentucky Irish American.
F459.L89I66 1995
070.4′42—dc20 95–7902

Contents

Foreword

It is surely worthwhile to save from oblivion the *Kentucky Irish American*, as Clyde Crews has done in this engaging book. Here are that weekly newspaper's comments on the political scene of the day in all their ferocious intensity, their unblinking partisanship, their clinical examination of the motives and the absurdities of office holders, mostly of course, Republicans—and the wit employed in their disembowelment. Mike Barry's pithy, sophisticated, discerning, and outrageous comments upon pols, public issues, and people are part of unsolemn Kentucky history. They are also very funny.

When Mike Barry died early in 1992, my son Barry commented that the *Irish American* was "the most amusing and insightful publication" he had ever read, and that Mike Barry was "certainly the most original journalist" he had ever met. After the demise of the *Irish American* in 1968, Mike wrote a popular sports column for the *Louisville Times*, from which he retired in 1984. But before he joined our newspapers, the "mausoleum at Sixth and Broadway" was fair game.

In spite of his unadmiring references to the *Courier-Journal* and the *Louisville Times*, I would sometimes feel a kind of envious admiration for Mike Barry as, defying the laws of libel, he would take out after his bêtes noires—more often than not, our bêtes noires, too. But the *Courier-Journal* rarely called George Wallace a louse or characterized Cardinal Cushing's accommodation of the John Birchers as "wedging his red-slippered foot back into his big mouth," or referred to Happy Chandler as "Blubber Boy" or to Richard Nixon as the "bum" or "Dickie Boy."

Over the years our differences with the *Irish American*'s views seemed to diminish. While Mike's father, John Barry, from whom Mike assumed the editorship in 1950, thought the League of Nations (which the *Courier-Journal* supported) so much "twaddle" and women's suffrage a mistake, Mike and the *Courier-Journal* agreed about the New Deal, defeating Hitler, civil rights, race relations, and, in time, about Vietnam.

Mike's uncompromising approach to every subject that engaged his zestful interest is nowhere more irresistible than in the letter he and his brother Joe, publisher of the *Irish American*, routinely sent to would-be subscribers. It read, in part:

> We appreciate your inquiry regarding this paper. The price of a year's subscription is $5. We cannot accept subscriptions for less than a year, nor do we make refunds to irate subscribers who wish to cancel when they discover their knotheaded opinions do not agree with our knotheaded opinions.
>
> It may save both time and trouble if you know, before you subscribe, some of our views. For instance, we despised Joe McCarthy when he was alive and we hate McCarthyism now. . . .
>
> We think Father Ginder, who writes in Our Sunday Visitor, is an incurable knucklehead. . . .
>
> Now that you have some idea, you may do as you please. It's your money.
>
> It's also our paper.

No matter what particular knuckleheadedness you as reader may harbor, could you resist sending in your five dollars?

This project grew from an earlier proposal by Jim Bolus and Billy Reed, sportswriters for our papers and close friends of Mike Barry, for support of the publication of a book focusing on Mike's sports column. A more comprehensive plan ensued: This anthology of editorials has been published, and the entire run of the *Kentucky Irish American* has been preserved on microfilm. The microfilmed collection will now be available for posterity and scholarly endeavors at the University of Louisville and the Louisville Free Public Library, while the yellowed and brittle originals will be carefully preserved at Bellarmine College. The Mary and Barry Bingham, Sr. Fund is pleased to support this book and the microfilmed collection.

The passage of time has softened, indeed, obliterated, my erstwhile feelings of resentment toward Mike Barry's barbs against the *Courier-Journal* (the "Curious Journal"). The wisdom and wit of the *Kentucky Irish American* form an element of our local history and culture that should live on in the public memory.

MRS. BARRY BINGHAM, SR.

Preface

The *Kentucky Irish American*, published in Louisville from 1898 to 1968, was a gadfly, a critic, a challenge—and a solace—for generations of Bluegrass Irish immigrants and their descendants. While it began as one of many such ethnic newspapers in America, it finished its days as much more. It came to represent a richly textured, sprightly, independent style of journalism read by a pluralistic audience of races and ethnicities—American all—throughout Kentucky and the nation.

From 1925 until its demise in 1968, the Barry family of Louisville owned, edited, and published the *Kentucky Irish American*. John J. Barry manned the editorial helm from 1925 until his death in 1950; his son Mike Barry succeeded him and remained until 1968. This anthology of editorial selections focuses on the Mike Barry years: nationally, from the cold war to the civil rights movement, and locally, on an era of special intensity in the unending political wars waged in the Commonwealth of Kentucky. The cast of characters is a large one that includes John F. Kennedy, Richard Nixon, Joseph McCarthy, Happy Chandler, Martin Luther King, Jr., and Barry Goldwater.

This collection of materials from the pages of the paper that the sage American sportswriter Red Smith called "all the excuse any man needs for learning to read" has come into existence through the encouragement and support of several thoughtful Kentuckians interested in preserving a unique journalistic heritage. In particular, I am grateful to Mrs. Barry Bingham, Sr., for the grant that made this research and writing possible.

Thanks are due also to Dr. Jay McGowan, president of

Bellarmine College, and Dr. David House, Bellarmine's academic vice-president, for providing the partial sabbatical that enabled the research to go forward. I offer my appreciation to the staffs of the Bellarmine College Library, the Louisville Free Public Library (Kentucky Division) and the University of Louisville Archives; to the late Mrs. Bennie Barry, Mr. James Barry, Mr. Joseph Barry, Dr. Mary Barry, Mr. Thomas ("Pete") Barry, Mr. Jim Bolus, Dr. John Gatton, Mr. Jack Malley, Mrs. Maureen McGowan, Mr. Rick Northern, Mr. Billy Reed, and Dr. Samuel W. Thomas, to Mr. Doug Thompson for research assistance; to Ms. Marquita Breit for her competent indexing work; and to my mother, Nell Crews, for proofreading assistance.

Editorial Note

Mike Barry generally wrote quite lengthy editorials for the *Kentucky Irish American* each week. In this anthology, excerpts have been reprinted from what were often considerably longer pieces. Paragraphs are reproduced intact as well as (it is hoped) the basic tenor of each article. The reader has been spared, however, a procession of ellipsis marks, especially at the conclusion of the selected editorials.

INTRODUCTION

A Brief History of the Kentucky Irish American

The First Fifty Years, 1898-1950

When the *Kentucky Irish American* first saw the light of journalistic day on the Fourth of July 1898, Louisville was one of the twenty largest cities in the nation, with a population twice that of Los Angeles or Atlanta, and four times that of Dallas or Houston. An industrial giant by southern standards, Louisville was linked to its Indiana shore town neighbors by railway bridge and ferry boat.[1]

The city boasted five daily newspapers (including the German-language *Anzeiger*), hundreds of houses of worship, lively theatrical and sporting offerings, a major league baseball team, and no fewer than seven foreign consuls. One of the finest park systems in the country, designed by Frederick Law Olmstead, had been developed during the decade of the 1890s.[2]

At the end of the nineteenth century, the "Falls City" was in many ways at least in the running for the distinction of being "the Boston of the South," according to New York journalist Arthur Krock.[3] Of course, Louisville was similar to Boston in that it had a considerable Irish immigrant population. But if it was Boston-like in its Irish and its amenities, Louisville was also "of the South" in its racial restrictions and attitudes. The recently dedicated (1895) Confederate Monument on Third Street towered

John J. Barry (1877-1950), editor of the *Kentucky Irish American* from 1925 to 1950. Courtesy of the Barry family.

over the South End to remind citizens of their southern sympathies.

Of the 204,000 residents of Louisville in this era, 4,200 had been born in Ireland. Counting first generation offspring, the Irish community approached 20,000.[4] According to the *Louisville Evening Post*, the Irish had become "almost pre-eminent" by the early twentieth century. Of the eminent "in medicine, at the bar, among the merchants, in the ministry, in music, in letters, in newspaper work," reported the *Evening Post*, most "have some Irish ancestry back of them. And they glory in it too."[5]

The weekly *Kentucky Irish American*, one of many such ethnic papers established across the nation during this era, likewise gloried in the Irish heritage of its readers. The paper's founder, William M. Higgins[6] (1852-1925), had moved to Louisville from Syracuse and had determined the patriotic founding date, July 4, to symbolize the paper's intention to be both proudly Irish and proudly American. His timing could hardly have been more auspicious, for the nation was in the midst of the Spanish-American War, and patriotism was at a fever pitch.

Also present at the *Irish American*'s inception was associate editor John J. Barry (1877-1950), who later would recall that there was literally dancing in the streets when the paper first appeared—because news had just arrived of the sinking of a Spanish fleet. Barry would become an increasingly dominant force at the paper, assuming the editorship after Higgins died suddenly on June 9, 1925, in the newspaper offices.[7]

John J. Barry had been born in the Limerick neighborhood of Louisville on July 22, 1877. The son of Michael Barry, a city police lieutenant, John Barry soon found himself involved in local Democratic politics. In time, he became treasurer for the Democratic County Executive Committee, and he served forty years as the city's Seventh Ward Democratic leader. He was a lifelong member of St. Louis Bertrand Church. At nineteen, Barry began a career in printing that was to eventuate in his affiliation with the *Irish American* from its beginning. Barry and his wife, Winifred Hennessy Barry, would raise nine children. The second-born, John Michael ("Mike"), assumed the editorship from his father when he died on February 8, 1950.[8]

The *Irish American* came to birth along old "Newspaper Row" in downtown Louisville at 319 Green Street. The Green Street name (apt, perhaps, for an Irish endeavor) would give way to the patriotic "Liberty Street" during World War I. The paper's offices remained there until 1966. At that time the offices, which had become a local legend for their dingy appearance and Old-World atmosphere, were moved to 325

St. Patrick's Day Parade in downtown Louisville, ca. 1919. Young Mike (in top hat) leads other enthusiastic Irish-American boys. Courtesy of the Barry family.

East Breckinridge Street from which the paper issued its final edition on November 30, 1968. Thus did the *Irish American* die at the biblical age of three score and ten.

In its earliest decades, there could be little mistaking the *Irish American*'s friends and enemies. It was Democratic, Irish, and Catholic. While it was never officially a religious paper, it reported to its heavily Roman Catholic audience on Catholic social events and presented features on the church and its leaders. The *Irish American* set out to instill pride in being both Catholic and American. It was always ready to rebut those who challenged Catholic patriotism or allegiance to American democracy. The Catholic Church, wrote the *Irish American* in 1918, is "the mother of civilization, of science, of learning, of education, of acts of charity and of love of the poor."[9]

Of course, the *Kentucky Irish American* was determined to keep a steady eye on local events. When a reformist, Fusionist ticket was formed to fight civic corruption in 1905, editor Higgins sneered at such "ranting mountebanks."[10] It applauded the gathering of the Louisville Literary Club at the Louisville Free Public Library in April, 1912, to discuss Irish poets and to hear local writer Madison Cawein lecture on the works of William Butler Yeats.[11]

With cinema becoming a growing cultural force, the *Irish American* thought that it could not be too morally vigilant. In 1921 it would congratulate the principal of St. Xavier for his efforts "to bring clean moving pictures" to the city. He had, said an editorial, kept "the children away from the Pickfords, Fairbanks, Chaplin and the other divorce court rotters."[12]

The paper's editorial policy was consistently pro-labor but anti-socialist.[13] Its most steady and consistent enemies included the Republican Party, the anti-immigrant American Protective Association, the Ku Klux Klan, Great Britain, and the *Courier-Journal* (which it perceived as pro-British and anti-Catholic).[14] When the Boer War ended in 1902, Higgins was convinced that the conflict had shown to the world "England's weakness, brutality and greed."[15]

During the second decade of the twentieth century, the *Irish American* would also strongly oppose prohibition, woman suffrage, and talk of a League of Nations, which it termed "silly twaddle."[16] Predictably, the paper was intent throughout World War I on expressing its intense patriotism, as expressed in its "Irish are Loyal" editorial the week of the American declaration of war.[17] It would cover extensively the 1916 Easter Rising in Ireland, but after the establishment of the Irish Free State in 1922, it would turn its attention less and less to Irish internal affairs.

The early *Irish American* was also quite capable of racism.

In 1919 it expressed the fear that Republicans sought to control the city "by an enormous negro vote."[18] In the spring of 1920 it had a field day mocking an African-American social event held "in the white folks' armory."[19] Such deplorable sentiments would make the paper's early and generally strong defense of the civil rights movement in the 1950s and 1960s all the more striking.

The controversy over Catholic presidential candidate Al Smith in 1928 brought forth some of the bluntest language in the *Irish American*'s repertoire. "Bigotry Won the Day" ran the headline in the edition after Herbert Hoover's election.[20] Enraged that heavily Democratic Kentucky had provided a 180,000 vote majority for Republican Hoover, the editor lashed out with a judgment that the Bluegrass State "will continue to stand before the world as the most bigoted and intolerant spot on the face of the earth." As a result of the election, "the Sacred Bill of Rights is nullified and the Catholic and the Jew are denied their political rights under the Constitution."[21]

The 1930s found the *Irish American* a staunch supporter of Franklin Roosevelt's New Deal. It supported Roosevelt at the end of the decade as he sought to strengthen the nation's military might, but it drew the line at American involvement overseas. An editorial written immediately after World War II began in Europe in September 1939 was titled "America First." Speaking of Hitler and his cohorts as "the madmen of Europe," Barry insisted to his readers, "We want none of their wars either over here or over there, and our preparedness will guarantee that policy."[22]

After Pearl Harbor, there were, of course, patriotic calls for unity and victory. Even more dramatic than any editorial that John Barry could write was a column he began publishing in April 1942 that ran weekly throughout the war. Called "Brothers in Arms," the column featured the letters home of Barry's sons from their military postings around the globe. Laced with insight and good humor, the column by 1944 had

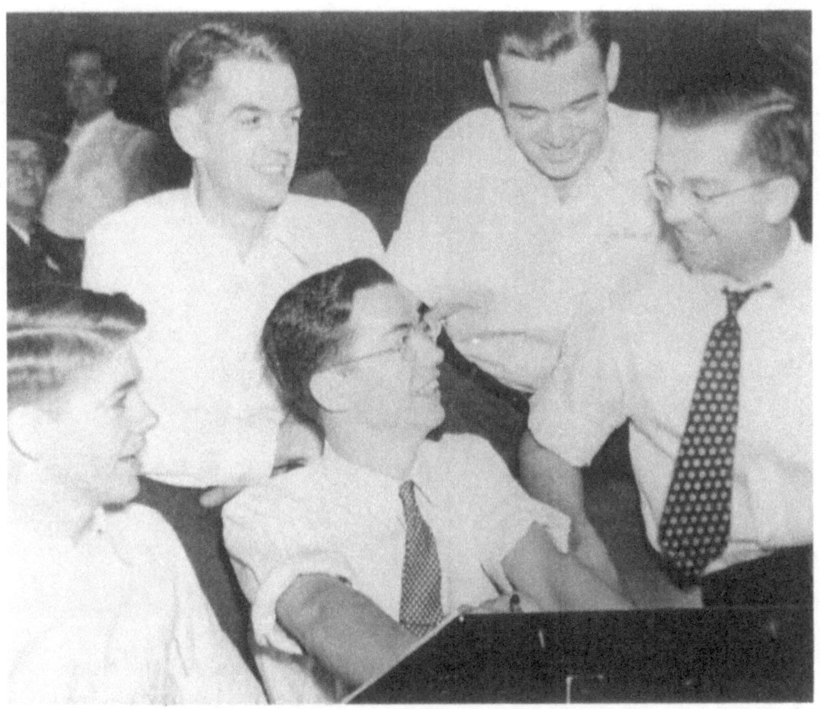

The Barry bowling team, December 20, 1941. Front row, left to right: Jim, Pete, and Mike; back row: Dan and Joe. Courtesy of the Barry family.

featured the writings of five of the Barry boys in uniform: Michael, Joseph, Daniel, Thomas, and James (Section 1).

By a serendipitous turn of events, son Michael was in Tokyo at the war's end, and in the course of an evening of "determined drinking" ran into *Courier-Journal* editor Barry Bingham, Sr. As a Japanese band played "My Old Kentucky Home," Navy Lieutenant Commander Bingham and Army Air Corps Captain Barry rose to sing all four verses at the tops of their lungs and received a thunderous round of applause.[23] Meanwhile, back home, editor John Barry was musing over the fate of the earth after the dropping of the

John J. and Winifred Barry with their family, taken in the front yard of their home at 633 West St. Catherine St., Louisville, in 1941. Back row, left to right: Mike, Joe, Dan, Mary Winifred, Mary Elizabeth, Mary Helen, William, Pete, and Jim. Courtesy of the Barry family.

first atomic bomb. "The human race," he wrote, "is at the crossroads. The atomic power must be used to prevent future wars or the world faces disaster."[24]

In 1948, Americans watched the Truman-Dewey presidential campaign with an air of predestination, generally convinced that Dewey was on his way to a smashing victory. Editor John Barry, an inveterate Democrat, was much more cautious, and in the event, more accurate as well. He wrote: "Here in Kentucky, where we remember even Man O' War was beaten, we think they'd better go ahead and have the race anyway."[25]

That same year of 1948, the *Irish American* paused to

celebrate its fiftieth year, and its friendly enemy, the *Courier-Journal*, produced a feature interview with the old editor. John J. Barry, the man who was known for his occasional ferociousness in print, surprised reporter Marion Porter by his mild manner. He even managed to say a few kindly things about a (very) few Republicans, while limiting his remarks about the *Courier-Journal* to the opinion that "it's just a little inconsistent."[26] When Barry died at his home at 633 St. Catherine Street, one block from the place of his birth, he had served in the *Irish American* editor's chair for twenty-five years. Flags at Louisville City Hall and the Jefferson County Court House were lowered in tribute.[27]

The Mike Barry Era, 1950-1968

The work of John Michael "Mike" Barry (1909-1992) had first appeared in the *Irish American* in September 1934 in a weekly back-page sports column. Assuming the identity of "the World's Greatest Handicapper," Barry and his sports column—except during the war years—would remain a staple of the *Irish American* for the rest of its existence. After 1957, the column would carry a signature photograph of Mike sitting cross-legged with his racing form, the sole of his shoe revealing a hole not unlike one made famous by Adlai Stevenson during his presidential campaigns.

Mike Barry was born in Louisville August 6, 1909, and graduated from St. Xavier High School. On December 7, 1941, that Sunday afternoon when Pearl Harbor was attacked, he was sitting in the family home on St. Catherine Street listening to the New York Philharmonic broadcast when a bulletin brought the news of the bombing. Like millions of others, his own life would be dramatically changed. Barry was to serve two years as a Captain with the 292nd Joint Assault Signal Operations Corps, 77th Division, in the Pacific. Shortly after his return, in January 1946, he married Benjamina (Bennie) Lancaster; eventually seven children would be born to the Barrys.[28]

Mike and famed trainer Mike Zito examine a copy of the *New Voice*. Courtesy of the Barry family.

Devout Catholics, the Barrys lived in Louisville's Highlands neighborhood. Mike generally read six newspapers daily, including the *Chicago Tribune* and the *New York Hearald-Tribune*. He was also an avid reader of Civil War history, biography, and popular fiction.

Barry was a Kentuckian with an intense love of his native commonwealth. Even when he traveled, Bennie Barry recalled, he kept his watch on Louisville time "because I want to know the time in Kentucky." At the time of his death, the family decided to bury him wearing his watch. "When he sees God," said his widow, "he will know what time it is in Kentucky." Bennie Barry herself would die during Derby Week 1994, and her obituary appeared in the *Courier-Journal* on Derby morning.

In addition to his work as editor of the *Irish American* from 1950 to 1968, Mike Barry would also serve in a variety of sports posts in his native city. He was sports commentator for WAVE radio and television and track announcer and odds maker for such now defunct racetracks as Miles Park and Louisville Downs. When the *Irish American* ceased publication in 1968, Barry took his journalistic skills over to Sixth and Broadway to become a sports writer for the *Courier-Journal* and *Louisville Times*. No one could have been more aware than Mike Barry of the irony that the long-time public critic of the *Courier-Journal* now wrote under its masthead. Barry would retire from the *Courier-Journal* in 1984, though he continued to write sports columns until the end of his life.

When it came to writing about the quintessential Kentucky sport of horse racing, Barry was to become a legend in his own time. He was, says sports author Jim Bolus, "the Dean of Derby writers. He knew more about Churchill Downs and the Kentucky Derby than anybody." Another well-known sports writer and historian, Billy Reed, called Barry "the last of a breed. I really don't think we're ever going to see his kind of personal journalism again." Dean Eagle of the *Louisville Times* spoke of Barry as "probably the best handicapper in Kentucky."[29]

To this day, many Louisvillians remember Mike Barry primarily as a sports writer, unaware that for eighteen years he provided incisive weekly commentary on local, national, and world affairs. Norman Isaacs, former managing editor of the *Louisville Times*, said of him: "Mike Barry is a fine writer with a marvelous touch for satire. He pricks the balloons of pomposity with almost unerring aim."[30]

Remaining in the editorial trenches as long as Mike Barry did—and writing with a style that was free-wheeling and often biting—inevitably brought critics in turn. When Mike Barry died in Louisville on January 10, 1992, an appreciative obituary used such words as "caustic," "crusty," and "testy" to describe his writing style. And yet, according to Francele Armstrong, writing in *Louisville Magazine* in 1966: "A fiery dragon in print, Mike in person is soft-spoken, charming and affable in the Barry family tradition."[31]

At the time of Mike Barry's death, Barry Bingham, Jr., former editor of the *Courier-Journal*, would attest that the *Kentucky Irish American* was "the most amusing and insightful publication I ever read." And its long-time editor Mike Barry, said Bingham, was "certainly the most original journalist I ever met." This, be it duly noted, came from a professional newspaper editor who had been around the journalistic block—and it was said of a man who had been one of the *Courier-Journal*'s most outspoken critics.[32]

In 1950, the first year of Mike Barry's editorship (with brother Joseph along as business manager), the United States entered the Korean War. The World War II veteran at first engaged in a bit of saber-rattling, urging the nation to go all out in its aggressiveness, but soon he came to a more temperate support of President Harry Truman's conduct of the conflict (Section 2). He quickly turned into a major critic of General Douglas MacArthur: "He just wants peace by enlarging the war, vast additions to our armed forces, and a cut in taxes, a facing up to our world responsibilities by withdrawing into isolation. It sure is a simple program, but you've got to have a simple mind not to see it's plumb ridiculous."[33]

Irish American editorials dealing with international problems in this early Cold War period could often take on an apocalyptic tone, with regular evocations of a cataclysmic third world war looming. Even such grim analysis could not prevent the Barry wit from surfacing. "Baseball in war time is supposed to keep up civilian morale," he wrote in the first summer of the Korean War. Then, mentioning a sagging Louisville team, he asked, "But what would you say the Colonels have been doing?"[34]

On the national political scene in the early 50s, Barry trained his sights on two targets in particular: Richard Nixon and Joseph McCarthy (Section 4). To the *Irish American*, Nixon as the new vice-president was "the bum" or "Dickie

Boy." The paper spoke of his weeping during his famous televised "Checkers" speech as "maudlin exhibition" and called Nixon "the Johnny Ray of politics,"[35] a reference to Ray's hit song entitled "Cry." As early as 1950, Barry criticized Wisconsin Senator Joseph McCarthy for his outrageous claims that Communists had infiltrated American life. A man himself attuned to the dangers of Communism, Barry by 1952 was calling McCarthy "the Wisconsin faker" and berating him for his "fantastic lies."[36]

Despite its immersion in Cold War politics, the *Irish American* paid attention to the situation in Ireland. An editorial headline in the summer of 1950 asserted, "*Courier-Journal* Again Attacks Ireland." The editorial concluded: "Every time the band plays 'America,' the *Courier-Journal* editorial staff stands up and sings 'God Save the King' "[37] (Section 9).

On the city scene, the *Irish American* continued its unyielding journalistic battles against that *other* paper, the *Courier-Journal*. Both the big city daily and the Democratic city administration, the *Irish American* was convinced, not only winked at vice in Louisville but were sanctimonious in the bargain (Section 8). Barry did not hesitate to entitle an editorial against the chief of police "Gets Dumber and Dumber."[38] And when a special investigator into corruption in city government resigned in 1951, Barry quipped: "He had to. His seeing eye dog died."[39]

Without a doubt, editor Barry saved up his most venomous barbs for the tortuous subject of statewide Kentucky politics. Extraordinary though it may seem to other Americans, Kentuckians have managed to turn their politics into a major league sport, rivaling even basketball for supremacy in the Bluegrass State. With elections held every six months according to the Commonwealth's constitution and electoral practices, the political trombones never have the chance to grow cold. The *Irish American* managed, throughout the Mike Barry years, to fill up its two long front-page editorial columns year-round with Kentucky political commentary and repartee.

The Bluegrass State is heavily Democratic at the state level, though it can often go Republican in national elections. Only one Republican, Louie Nunn, served a term as governor in Kentucky in the fifty years after World War II. This means, of course, factions within the Democratic Party. In the 1950s and early 1960s, this meant the wings headed by A.B. "Happy" Chandler on one side and Earle Clements and Bert Combs on the other. These represented, respectively and broadly-speaking, a conservative versus a liberal approach to government.[40]

Although Barry the father had maintained friendly (though at times critical) relations with Chandler during his first term as governor (1935-39), Barry the son devoted more ink to Chandler's vilification than to any other subject (Section 5). Chandler was successful in his second bid to be governor winning the primary on August 6, 1955, thereby insuring his election in November. This was a "catastrophe,"[41] Barry charged, to be equated with the dropping of the first atomic bomb ten years earlier to the day. Kentucky immediately became "occupied" territory. Barry wrote: "Years from now—you should live so long—you may be asked what you did during the occupation of 1955–59, when you were a resident of the rebel stronghold of Jefferson County."[42] Small wonder that Chandler has no love for residents of Louisville and Jefferson County, the *Irish American* insisted. "They have regularly demonstrated that they know him for the fat fraud he is."[43] In the summer of 1956, speculation surfaced that the Kentucky governor might be nominated for president, at least as a "favorite son" candidate. "Where the heck's the un-American Activities Committee?" Barry wondered from his Liberty Street fortress. "If that's not a downright subversive statement, we never heard one."[44]

As the convention neared, the Chandler candidacy talk continued unabated. The stage was set for what was to become the best remembered and most quoted remark of

Barry's long career: "Any time Chandler is referred to in Chicago as 'Kentucky's favorite son,' it should be made unmistakably clear that the sentence is incomplete."[45] Later that summer of 1956, Chandler was speech-making in Iowa when Barry asked his readers, "The biggest corn-producing state in the union has to import more?"[46] During another stump speech, Chandler, in a biblical frame of mind, had remarked: "Goodness and kindness have followed me all the days of my life." The *Irish American* snapped back, "Don't worry, they'll never catch up."[47]

Although Mike Barry spent a good deal of editorial lineage calling Happy Chandler names, he could at more analytical moments present a reasoned set of objections to specific Chandler statements or policies. Perhaps, most notable was Chandler's claim to have been responsible for the racial integration of major league baseball during his term as Baseball Commissioner. Barry also insisted that Chandler had flirted with the Dixiecrats in 1948, that he had removed the state Board of Health from Louisville to Frankfort, and that he had raised state taxes.[48]

When the *Irish American* announced its closing in 1968, Happy Chandler sent a sporting letter of good wishes and Barry responded with a set of corrective footnotes to Chandler's epistle. Readers seeking an objective and less emotional glance at the career of A.B. ("Happy") Chandler may consult the 1992 *Kentucky Encyclopedia*.[49]

With Chandler out of office (after 1959) and the presidential election of 1960 on the horizon, the *Irish American* could turn its attention again more steadily to national political issues. Surprisingly for an Irish Catholic writer, some would think, Mike Barry was not an early supporter of John Fitzgerald Kennedy. Rather, he supported the candidacy of Adlai Stevenson of Illinois, calling the Massachusetts senator "too young and too Catholic."[50] Even a personal letter from Kennedy (printed in the *Irish American*) failed to charm the editor into a change of mind.[51] (Section 6).

By the campaign of 1960, of course, the paper was solidly

The Barry's Christmas card for 1958 shows "the world's greatest handicapper at home" with wife Bennie (right) and daughters. Courtesy of the Barry family.

behind the Democratic nominee. The local Baptist paper, the *Western Recorder*, produced a series of articles questioning the appropriateness of having a Catholic in the White House.[52] Barry reminded Catholic readers that many Protestants across the land had been courageous in responding to such challenges: "They have steadfastly refused to take the easier road of silence."[53] Still, when Kennedy was inaugurated in January 1961, Barry could not resist quipping, "It may be weeks before he can get construction started on that tunnel to the Vatican." He also remarked on the new president's "magnificent" inaugural address.[54]

Throughout the Kennedy years, the *Irish American* generally supported JFK's policies, including his handling of the Cuban Missile Crisis and his proposals for the limitations of nuclear weapons. When the young president was slain in Dallas, Barry produced a moving eulogy: "There was a wake in every house along the block, on all the streets of all the towns over all this grieving land."[55]

In local politics in the 1960s Mike Barry had a new list of political villains at whom to strike: Louie Nunn, governor of Kentucky (1967-71), whom he bluntly called a racist and the "Typhoid Mary" of Kentucky politics,[56] and Gene Snyder, the Louisville-area congressman whom he routinely referred to as "M. Genius Snyder."[57]

The *Irish American* also gingerly approached the overriding national concern of the Vietnam War. As early as 1965 it cautioned against American involvement in an Asian ground war: "This is precisely the mess we're in now."[58] But on balance, like many another publication in the nation at this stage of the war, the paper did little more than wring its editorial hands. Of Vietnam, the editor wrote, "We have a terrible problem for which no one has a solution. So until one is found, we have no choice but to continue on our present course."[59] When President Lyndon Johnson ordered a cessation of bombing in 1968, the paper applauded his decision.[60]

By far the issue of the 1960s on which the *Irish American* was most outspoken was the civil rights movement (Section 7). Even in the last days of John J. Barry's editorship in 1949, the paper had begun to reprint national articles favorable to "Negro rights."[61] In 1950, under Mike Barry's leadership, the paper had called on local Democrats to run a Negro for a seat on the Board of Aldermen.[62] As the civil rights movement grew locally and nationally in the 1960s, Barry's editorial voice spoke out in favor of legislation to afford equal civic rights and dignities to all races.

In Louisville, the civil rights movement centered around a major legislative battle over an open accommodations law in 1963, and an even bitterer battle over an open housing ordinance in 1967. An aldermanic vote in the spring of 1967 resulted in the ordinance's rejection by a vote of 9-3. Barry quickly dubbed the majority aldermen "the nine hunks of solid concrete."[63] What the open housing problem needs in Louisville, he wrote, "is a few open minds, and that is precisely what we've got damned few of."[64] After an intensive election campaign in the fall of the same year, a new Board of Aldermen passed the open housing measure readily.

A general supporter of Dr. Martin Luther King, Jr., Barry became disillusioned with the civil rights leader after a speech in which he proclaimed America the greatest aggressor in the world.[65] When Dr. King was assassinated in April 1968, Barry chose not to run an obituary. Rather, he offered a black-bordered box on the front page with this King quotation: "All men are created equal. Not some men. Not white men. All men. America, rise up and come home."[66]

By the fall of 1968, with printing costs rising and with Barry wearied perhaps by the burden of producing a weekly with only a minimal staff, the *Kentucky Irish American* matter-of-factly reported its own upcoming demise in a simple boxed front-page announcement. There were not cosmic farewells. Appreciative articles from the *Courier-Journal* were reprinted in final editions. The next-to-last issue, dated November 23, 1968, had an over-header reading "Penultimate Issue." The final issue, of November 30 1968, was business as usual, the regular columns appearing without farewells.

In its last year, the paper had begun to feature a boxed quotation from a notable historical figure on each front page. In August, no doubt reflecting the editor's own somber uneasiness with the modern American mindset, the historian Gibbon was quoted about the fall of Athens: "In the end, more than they wanted freedom, they wanted security. They wanted a comfortable life and lost it all—security, comfort and freedom. When the Athenians finally wanted not to give to society, but for society to give to them, when the freedom they wished for was freedom from responsibility, then Athens ceased to be free. . . ."[67]

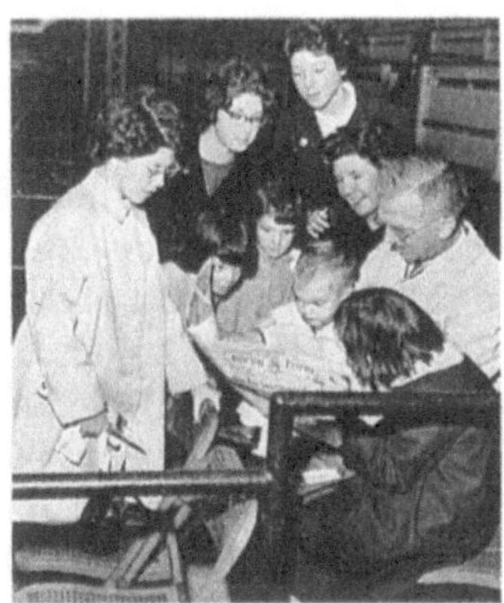

By Christmas 1962, Jack had been added to the family. That year the Barrys' Christmas card proclaimed: "The family that bets together . . . frets together!" Photos by Mode, courtesy of the Barry family.

For its final quotation on November 30, 1968, the *Irish American* turned to Abraham Lincoln and thus indirectly said its farewell with a reassuring bit of philosophic common sense: "Human nature will not change. In any future great national trial, compared with the men of this time, we shall have as weak and as strong, as silly and as wise, as bad and as good."[68]

And so, while America endured the discord and strife of 1968, that tumultuous year of confrontation, disillusionment, protests, riots, and assassinations, the *Kentucky Irish American* slipped into history after seventy years of life. It had been one of the last ethnic Irish papers in America to survive, leaving behind only a handful, such as the *Irish Echo* in New York City.[69]

In its palmiest days, in the middle of the twentieth century, circulation was estimated at some 4,000 to 5,000 on both its local and its national mailing lists. The paper in 1966 was mailed to forty-three states; its subscribers included Harry Truman, Franklin D. Roosevelt, Jr., and Robert Wagner, former mayor of New York City.

Only a memory now are the years when all of the Barry boys, who had once been "Brothers in Arms"—Mike, Joe, Tom (a.k.a. "Pete"), Jim, and Dan—would mount the rickety stairs on Liberty Street to aid in dispatching the weekly fusillade of 7,000 words packed into the paper's four pages. (After 1955, Mike Barry's daughters—Jane, Kate, Winnie, Mary, and Julie—served their time, yet another generation helping with the newspaper.) Absent from the Louisville scene is perhaps the only newspaper in America with the policy of publishing only critical letters to the editor—never fulsome ones. When the *Irish American* began to run music reviews by a local attorney, Robert Burke, Jr., a man with a hearing aid, a nasty salvo came from a reader and ended up on page 1: "What paper but the *Irish American* would hire a deaf music editor?"[70]

Never again would sound the stinging editorial ripostes. Never again would appear the columns on horses or bowling or the scholarly reviews of classical music concerts that had been part of the paper's pride. Never again would be printed the famous annual "green ink issue" during the week of St. Patrick's Day that featured a map of Ireland with the locations of famous families. Gone was a Louisville journalism institution, and a critic to generations.

The *Louisville Times* proved itself to be particularly gracious in a farewell editorial:

For 70 years the witty fiery weekly . . . has delighted, deflated and bruised with a fine and free-swinging style of personal journalism seldom seen today in our land. Armed with little more than a

1898 – 71st YEAR OF PUBLICATION – 1968

KENTUCKY IRISH AMERICAN

ESTABLISHED JULY 4, 1898 VOL. CXXXIX, No. 18 LOUISVILLE, SATURDAY, MAY 4, 1968 PRICE TEN CENTS

UPSTAGED

CANDIDATES CAN'T CAMPAIGN AGAINST FLOOD OF DERBY TALK

ROCKEFELLER'S ANNOUNCEMENT RENEWS RUMOR OF REAGAN PAIRING

NEXT TUESDAY IN INDIANA VITAL TO BOTH KENNEDY, McCARTHY

Whether they wanted to or not, and with the primary only a little over three weeks away they didn't want to, all of the many candidates in Kentucky have had to cease and desist from campaigning the past week. It just hasn't been possible for them to interest the voters in war or peace or taxes or schools or anything else.

Anything, that is, except the one subject that interests most Kentuckians the first week in May.

If any one candidate had the nerve to gamble, he could do a lot of campaigning this week by promising to give his listeners the Derby winner. Obviously this is a gamble—if he told them they could get the rent money on a horse that finished at the eighth pole, he would have to withdraw.

But suppose this brave soul actually delivered? It would convince a lot of people he was a man of rare judgment.

The idea is offered here free to any candidate who wants it. Please note only the idea is offered—not the vital information the candidate needs to carry it out.

IN, OUT, BACK IN

On the national scene, the big news is Rockefeller's decision to get back into the presidential race. The New York governor has gotten about as easy to predict as one of those Churchill Downs races with a dozen 3 and 4-year-old maidens—when you expect him to announce his candidacy, Rocky goes on national television and says he's not going to run.

Then, when newsmen press him about his availability for a draft, Rockefeller gives them a definite maybe.

Anyway, as of now he's back in. Those Republicans who have been convinced their party would be a sure winner in November if they could run someone other than Nixon can now take heart. If a Republican wants to be against Tricky Dick, he now has someplace to go.

The GOP "dream ticket" of Rockefeller and Reagan has a chance—not a good one but a chance—of blocking the Nixon steamroller at the Miami Beach convention. With the New York governor to cut into the Democratic and Independent vote, and the California governor to add glamor to the campaign, this coast-to-coast hookup might appear an attractive package to the Republican delegates.

PROBLEMS PILING UP AT HOME

While Reagan has indicated he isn't at all interested in running for Vice President, or in being No. 2 to anybody, it's possible the tax reaction in California will change his mind.

Ronnie boy's people have just been hit with a billion-dollar increase in state taxes. "Many in the middle income brackets," writes Marquis Childs, "found their tax bill upped three to four times." (This is reminiscent of Chandler's second term here some ten years ago, when middle income people had their state income tax boosted 50 per cent and then had to listen to Chandler's boast that he had cut taxes.)

Childs added, "Reagan can blame much of his on his predecessor, Edmund G. (Pat) Brown, who in the last years of his second term used every possible device to postpone the evil day.

"Yet, as the pressures of the office bear down harder and harder, with the prospect of even higher levies just ahead, Reagan is increasingly restive and uneasy. He is starting soon on what is close to an open campaign for the presidency. Using that convenient euphemism 're-assess' to describe his attitude, Reagan is moving from noncandidate to a modest political striptease.

"In May he is speaking in three states, accompanied for the first time by reporters in a chartered jet, four times in Florida, once in Cleveland and Chicago. As of now, his associates say, he is not going into Oregon to campaign for the May 28 primary where his name is on the ballot. But his wealthy backers are putting a sizeable chunk of money into the state, most of it for television. . .

"No one can deny Reagan's chief political claim—he is the party's star fund raiser, a vaudeville turn packing them in on the whole circuit. This might well mean the reward of second place on the Republican ticket. Reagan has repeatedly said he is not interested in the vice presidency. But a draft by the convention would take him out of an office more and more burdensome and frustrating and with very little future. . .

"New" Speech is Frightening

"For his forthcoming tour, Reagan is polishing a new speech. He tried it out in Phoenix on April 9. Let's avoid the temptation of an election year, he told a dinner audience, leave the promises of an unreachable Utopia to the opposition. . .

> *"Describe the Kentucky Derby? If I could do that, I'd have a larynx of spun silver and the tongue of an anointed angel."*
>
> —*Irvin S. Cobb*

"In the same speech he warned against losing the Vietnam war at the conference table. . . He demanded to know why we had not recovered the Pueblo and its crew with force if necessary. But that is the variety Ronnie's audiences have come to expect from a performer with such notable professional skill."

As Childs indicates, Reagan's new speech doesn't make any more sense than his old one—he says the party shouldn't make any unreachable promises and in the next breath suggests getting the Pueblo and its crew back would be a simple matter for a firm executive.

Get the ship and the sailors back "by force, if necessary," Ronnie says.

Now there's a brilliant suggestion from a man who thinks he's qualified for the Presidency, and who could end up just a heartbeat away from the job.

Use what force? And where? And how? And what would the final price be if we ever did get the ship and the men back by force?

But, as another writer points out, Reagan speaks "to audiences essentially incurious because their main demand is not to be disturbed."

Maybe Ronnie's listeners aren't disturbed, but those who examine the content of his speeches certainly are.

ACROSS THE RIVER, "SUDDEN DEATH"

Neither candidate is saying so, but next Tuesday's presidential primary in Indiana is what they call overtime games in pro football—"sudden death." If Robert Kennedy loses to McCarthy, that'll be all for Bobby, and if McCarthy takes a beating the man from Minnesota can forget future primaries and go back to his Senate duties.

The thing about McCarthy is that all the experts have been saying he's a great guy and would make a fine President—but he can't be elected. When McCarthy got the votes he did in New Hampshire, the same experts said he wasn't running against anybody.

Therefore, if McCarthy loses next Tuesday, the experts will say they were right all along and goodbye, Gene, it was nice knowing you.

A win for Kennedy is a must for his campaign. There are already a lot of Democrats who have been saying they're delighted to see Hubert Humphrey get into the race, when what they really mean is they don't like Bobby and will take any reasonable alternative — but if Kennedy is really strong they don't want to be left out in the cold.

Naturally, if Bobby stumbles, there'll be a mad rush to the Humphrey bandwagon.

The guess here is that Kennedy will win in Indiana, although perhaps by not enough to really discourage the Humphrey camp.

NOTES

Rockefeller says he's getting into the race because he's "deeply disturbed at the growing unrest and anxiety at home." Did he mean at home in his Republican Party when they thought of being stuck with Nixon? . . . When you read the letters-to-the-editor column in any paper in the country, you get the impression every radical right nut must write at least one letter before breakfast . . . A man said you could tell there were some strange drivers in town this week — he saw one give the right of way to pedestrians in a cross-walk . . . President Johnson began a recent state dinner talk with this Liberian proverb: "A man who is asked to talk an inch and speaks a yard should be given a foot." . . . The trouble with staging the Belle of Louisville-Delta Queen boat race is that the promoters can't arrange a boat race . . . Smartest idea of the week was to name Jimmy Ellis grand marshal of the parade . . . Drive-in theater operators are crying over daylight saving time, but before you cry along with them in sympathy just remember these are the people who inflict commercials on a captive audience and have long intermissions to build up their concession business . . . The happiest Derby party of all will be the line at the cashiers' windows.

WHAT WAR WAS THIS?

(Carteret County News-Times, Morehead City, N.C.)

"Worst of all division of sentiment in the nation. In New England church bells were tolled and flags hung at half mast when the declaration of war was announced. Massachusetts, Rhode Island, and Connecticut refused to allow their militia to be ordered out as Congress required, and during the entire war the New England section, which had accumulated half the specie of the country, did all in its power to obstruct the financial operations of the government . . .

". . . The government was nearly bankrupt, the blockade having cut off almost all the revenue from customs duties, and New England having refused to contribute from its horde of specie to the purchase of loans. The last loan offered had failed, and all banks south of Connecticut had suspended specie payment . . .

". . . Disaffection to the national government had been steadily increasing. Many acts of both governors and legislatures can hardly be regarded as less than traitorous . . ."

The quotations are from James Truslow Adams's history of the United States, "The March of Democracy, War of 1812."

MOTORCYCLE HELMETS

(Commercial Appeal)

Last year the motorcycle death rate declined 27 per cent. It was the first time there had been a reduction in six years. Deaths went down in the face of a rise of 438,000 in the number of cycles. The point is that 30 states now require a motorcyclist to wear a helmet.

The one-year reduction in deaths in New York State was 50 per cent. By contrast, California still allows bare heads and had an increase of 9 per cent in deaths. This kind of figure ought to bring the number of helmet states to 50 in short order.

FIRST PICK

A kind-hearted man used to bring home some of the worst looking bums to give them a square meal. His wife fed them all, but one night she said, "Why do these bums you bring home always have to be so dirty?"

The man said, "The clean ones, the rich people get!"

ST. FRANCES FISH FRY NEXT FRIDAY

The St. Frances of Rome PTA will sponsor a fish fry next Friday, May 10, with serving beginning at 5 o'clock. Carry-out service will be available, and there will be games and refreshments for both adults and children. Proceeds will go for the education improvement fund.

LOVE O' HOMELAND!

Damon Runyon's Famous Piece on 1926 Derby Still a Classic

A strange regret came over me when Bubbling Over, the Kentucky horse, won the Kentucky Derby at Churchill Downs, and I stood witness to the most tremendous display of human enthusiasm I have ever witnessed.

I saw silvery haired old ladies, their faces bright and shining, fairly shivering with joy. I saw old men, with weather-beaten faces, leaning forward breathlessly, eyes glowing fiercely, and lips moving. I saw exultant-looking citizens standing with fists hard lifted to the sky as if trying to drive them through some unseen opposition overhead. I heard their voices booming.

I saw beautiful girls, flushed, disheveled with excitement and nervous agitation, their delicate fingers clutching, their voices shrilling.

I saw young men fairly jumping up and down in an excess of joy, yelling hoarse shouts. I heard the cries of little children.

And seeing this, and hearing this, I thought to myself, standing there: "Old boy, it must be a wonderful thing to be a Kentuckian at this moment!"

And that was the moment of my regret, and my regret was over not being born and raised down there in Kentucky, that I might feel in my heart the joy of these people and be a party to their enthusiasm.

I got my little thrill just from the spectacle of the race, to be sure. I always get some thrill out of these things. But it didn't exactly stir my soul. It didn't reach down into the very depths, as it did with these people, and bring out in one sudden blast of emotion that amounted to a fury that very wonderful emotion—LOVE O' HOMELAND!

I tell you I envied those Kentuckians!

I felt quite alien, and very much of an outsider as their common joy swept them together in one glittering phalanx of pride, and they seemed to face the rest of us, standing there a bit silent, and bewildered—seemed to face us with an air of triumphant arrogance, as much to say:

"Why you poor fish!"

But I didn't feel any tinge of resentment. I merely felt regret. I regretted I hadn't even bet on the Bradley stable to win the Derby, that I might have at least a sort of non-resident share in the Kentucky enthusiasm.

Now then, you may say a horse race is a mighty little thing to produce all this fuss.

If you say that, you do not understand, and not understanding it is useless to argue with you.

There was in that outburst, not only Kentucky's joy over a Kentucky victory in a horse race, but Kentucky's defiance to these who had planned to steal one little mite of Kentucky's prestige, whether represented by men or horses.

Behind it was the same general sentiment that rallies Kentuckians to arms against a foe. That Kentucky crowd didn't see only the Kentucky horses, Bubbling Over and Bagenbaggage galloping there in front of the colors of the East. It saw the glory of Kentucky spread before alien eyes like a banner in the sky.

I say to you here that I love every blade in the Blue Grass because of the loyalty of Kentuckians to Kentucky; because of their pride of race. I despise the man who speaks disparagingly of his home town, or his home State—the professional non-homer, which has become a familiar type in some parts of the land, although I rather doubt that he exists in Kentucky.

My neat, but gaudy made-in-Baltimore straw hat is lifted once more to Kentucky in something more than the casual gesture.

I have said before in this column that the Kentucky Derby is the greatest of all the American sports spectacles, but I was never before fortunate enough to see it as a real Kentucky victory, with Kentucky horses running one-two.

I am inclined to think that the demonstration over Bubbling Over—they refer to him in Kentucky as "Bubblin'," and over Bagenbaggage, too, was "tops" as the boys say in fervor, and in reflecting something more real, more genuine in feeling than mere delight in winning a bet.

It's a great State, Kentucky. They're great people, Kentuckians.

And they've got great horses down there, too.

Damon Runyon—1926

The Derby Day edition of May 4, 1968, a few months before the *KIA* ceased publication. Courtesy of the Barry family.

typewriter, an uncertain list of subscribers, a love of the language and an instinct for human comedy, Mike Barry made a career of puncturing stuffed shirts . . . .

Not that Mike Barry was always caustic; his obituaries for departed friends had the ring of the sweet keening of an Irish minstrel at a wake. His praise was doubly sweet for its rarity and the deftness of its expression. And always what he wrote, in indignation or sorrow or savage attack, was his own, personal and proud, and touched with the humor that was at the heart of the man and his work.[71]

One anecdote that made the rounds at the time of the *Irish American*'s closing was of an editor at the *Wall Street Journal* who met a Louisvillian and remarked, "So you're from Louisville, home of the great newspaper." "Yes," the Kentuckian replied, "you mean the *Courier-Journal*." "No," said the editor, "I mean the *Irish American*."[72]

Perhaps the greatest valedictory of all was spoken by one of America's most famous sportswriters, Red Smith: "Around our house the *Kentucky Irish American* rates above bread and just below whiskey as one of the necessities of life. It's all the excuse any man needs for learning to read."[73]

Notes

Abbreviations: *CJ* Courier-Journal;
KIA *Kentucky Irish American;*
LT *Louisville Times*

1. For population figures, see *The World Almanac and Book of Facts* 1988, 538. See also CJ March 20, 1926.
2. *Caron's Louisville Directory for 1898, passim.*
3. Arthur Krock, *Myself When Young* (Boston: 1973), 187.
4. Stanley Ousley, Jr., *The Irish in Louisville*, M.A. thesis, Univ. of Louisville, 1974. This is an extremely helpful resource in the study of Irish history in Kentucky's largest city. See especially its fourth chapter, "The *Kentucky Irish American*." The thesis is available in the University of Louisville Ekstrom Library.
5. *Louisville Evening Post*, March 16, 1910.
6. See obituaries of William M. Higgins in the *CJ* and the

Louisville Herald, June 10, 1925. Another early associate editor was Bernard Cavanaugh. *CJ*, June 22, 1948.

7. "Barry to Mark 50th Year with Paper," *CJ*, June 22, 1948.

8. *LT*, Feb. 8, 1950. The Barry children and their years of birth were: Mary Elizabeth (1907), John Michael (1909), Joseph Thomas (1911), Daniel Dominic (1913), William Thomas (1916), Mary Winifred (1918), Mary Helen (1920), Thomas Patrick (1922), and James Luke (1925).

9. *KIA*, November 23, 1918.

10. *KIA*, Sept. 30, 1905. For a detailed study of the reformist struggle in local politics during this era, see George Yater, *200 Years at the Falls of the Ohio* (Louisville: 1987), 146 ff. The Kentucky Court of Appeals in 1907 invalidated the Louisville election of 1905.

11. *KIA*, April 27, 1912.

12. *KIA*, Jan. 29, 1921.

13. Ousley, 93.

14. *KIA*, Feb. 16, 1901: "The *Courier-Journal* has slandered the Catholics at every opportunity." In its issue of March 15, 1902, the *KIA* took to task a *Louisville Times* article for its tone in reporting the arrival of relics at St. Martin's Church in Louisville.

15. *KIA*, June 7, 1902.

16. *KIA*, Nov. 22, 1919. For an editorial against woman suffrage, see the issue of March 30, 1912. *Courier-Journal* editor Henry Watterson had a powerful objection to woman suffrage as well. He called suffrage supporters "silly Sallies and crazy Janes." See Arthur Krock, ed., *The Editorials of Henry Watterson* (Louisville: 1923), 358. See also Watterson's major statement on the topic, "The Most Momentous Question of Modern Times," *CJ*, Aug. 24, 1913.

17. *KIA*, April 7, 1917.

18. Ousley, 107. *KIA*, Oct. 18, 1919.

19. For a vivid description of segregated life in Louisville in this era, see George C. Wright, *Life behind a Veil* (Baton Rouge, 1985). See also his more recent work, *Racial Violence in Kentucky* (Baton Rouge, 1990).

20. *KIA*, Nov. 10, 1928. For coverage of Catholics in Kentucky and the 1928 presidential election, see Clyde F. Crews, *An American Holy Land* (Wilmington, 1987), 243-46.

21. Ousley, 106; *KIA*, Nov. 10, 1928.

22. *KIA*, Sept. 16, 1939.

23. *KIA,* Oct. 13, 1945.
24. *KIA,* Aug. 18, 1945.
25. *KIA,* July 17, 1948.
26. "Barry to Mark 50 Years, *CJ*, June 22, 1948.
27. *CJ*, Feb. 8, 1950.
28. "Caustic Longtime Louisville Writer Mike Barry Dies," *CJ*, Jan. 11, 1992. Most of the biographical material in this and the following three paragraphs comes from this obituary, as well as the author's interview with Bennie Barry, June 3, 1993. For the Pearl Harbor reference, see *KIA*, May 20, 1944.

The seven Barry children are: Jane, Catherine, Winifred, Mary, Julie, Anne, and John Michael, Jr. In the interview of June 3, 1993, Bennie Barry confirmed that as far as she knew the *KIA* was never sued. Mike had given his own reason for this earlier: "People knew the [Barry] brothers didn't have any money." *CJ* Jan. 11, 1992.

Bennie Barry was an accomplished professional in real estate and an active leader in the Audubon Society. She died in Louisville on May 5, 1994. *CJ*, May 7, 1994.

For an appreciative view of Mike Barry as sportsman, see the chapter on Barry in Jim Bolus, *Kentucky Derby Stories,* (Gretena, La., 1993). See also Bolus's piece on Barry, "On His Own Turf," *Business First*, March 30, 1992.

29. For Bolus and Reed quotations, see obituary of Jan. 11, 1992. The Dean Eagle quote is to be found in Jim Morrissey, "Mike Barry's Personal Newspaper," *Catholic Digest*, Oct. 1961, 126.
30. Morrissey, 124.
31. Francele Armstrong, "Mike Barry, Editor Unbridled," *Louisville Magazine*, Jan. 1966, 26.
32. *CJ*, Jan. 11, 1992.
33. *KIA*, Aug. 4, 1951.
34. *KIA*, Aug. 26, 1950.
35. *KIA*, Sept. 27, 1952; Nov. 22, 1952.
36. *KIA*, Nov. 8, 1952.
37. *KIA*, Aug. 26, 1950.
38. *KIA*, Sept. 13, 1952.
39. *KIA*, April 7, 1951.
40. For an extensive study of Kentucky politics in these years, see John Ed Pearce, *Divide and Dissent: Kentucky Politics,1930-1967* (Lexington, 1987). See also William Ellis, "Democratic Party," *The Kentucky Encyclopedia* (Lexington, 1992), 260-62.

41. *KIA*, June 1, 1963. Barry often returned to this theme. August 6 was the date of the anti-immigrant riots in Louisville in 1855 that killed over twenty people. It was the date in 1945 on which the atomic bomb was dropped on Hiroshima, and the date of Chandler's primary victory in 1955, making his second term as governor possible. The date had a way of sticking in the editor's memory: it was also his birthday.

42. *KIA*, March 8, 1958.

43. *KIA*, March 15, 1958.

44. *KIA*, May 12, 1956.

45. *KIA*, June 16, 1956.

46. *KIA*, July 14, 1956.

47. *KIA*, Feb. 14, 1959. Barry quoted this again in his year-end review, Jan. 20, 1960.

48. *KIA*, March 1, 1958.

49. *KIA*, Nov. 23, 1968. The Chandler entry in *The Kentucky Encyclopedia* (179) was written by Lowell Harrison.

50. *KIA*, Nov. 8, 1958.

51. *KIA*, March 28, 1959.

52. The *Western Recorder*, Sept. 29, 1960, for example, commented: "It's not the candidate but Catholicism we fear. For some it's not even American Catholicism, but religion *à la Rome* which is feared." See also a *Western Recorder* article of Oct. 27, 1960, reporting on the numerical growth of Catholics in America.

53. *KIA*, Nov. 5, 1960.

54. *KIA*, Nov. 12, 1960; Jan. 28, 1961.

55. *KIA*, Nov. 30, 1963.

56. *KIA* Nov. 4, 1967; Nov. 9, 1963. Lowell Harrison has produced an objective study of Nunn in *The Kentucky Encyclopedia*, 685-86.

57. *KIA*, Nov. 7, 1964. Barry had special praise for Kentucky Congressman Carl Perkins of Hindman. While some of Kentucky's congressional delegation—Barry called them "gutless wonders"—voted against the Civil Rights Act of 1964, Perkins "was man enough to stand up for the rights of all Americans." Ibid.

58. *KIA*, July 17, 1965.

59. *KIA*, Feb. 5, 1966.

60. *KIA*, April 6, 1968.

61. *KIA*, Feb. 5, 1949.

62. *KIA*, Dec. 30, 1950.

63. *KIA*, April 29, 1967.

64. *KIA*, March 18, 1967.

65. *KIA*, "King Abdicates," April 8, 1967.

66. *KIA*, April 13, 1968.

67. *KIA*, Aug. 3, 1968.

68. *KIA*, Nov. 30, 1968.

69. Ousley, 86. The 1966 circulation figure comes from Armstrong, 26-27. For references to famous readers of the *KIA*, see Morrissey, 123-28.

70. Morrissey, 124, 128. This article also quotes a Barry editorial opposing a "Catholic seat" on the U.S. Supreme Court. "The Supreme Court should be made up of the nine most qualified men in the country. If these men happen to be all Catholics, or all Protestants, or all Jews, or any mixture of all three, it should make no difference" (128). When this article resulted in a deluge of national requests for subscriptions, Mike and Joe Barry prepared a snappy form letter telling would-be subscribers what they were getting themselves into (Section 9). Music editor Burke, for the record, was neither deaf nor salaried.

71. *Louisville Times*, Nov. 16, 1968.

72. "Peppery *Irish American* Will End Publication," *CJ*, Nov. 15, 1968.

73. Ibid. In the same issue of the *CJ*, a separate article was entitled "Few Things Were Sacred to the *Irish-American*."

THE KENTUCKY IRISH AMERICAN

Excerpts from Selected Editorials from the Mike Barry Years

1

A Brother in Arms

The years of American involvement in World War II brought an unusual number of grim reports of battles and massive death to *Irish American* columns. The sprightly commentary on Kentucky politics continued unabated all the same.

By 1944, editor John J. Barry's five sons—Michael, Joseph, Daniel, Thomas, and James—were serving in the American armed forces. In that same year, the year that brought the D-Day invasion of Normandy, the liberation of Rome, and the Battle of the Bulge, one of the most popular and eagerly awaited columns in the *Irish American* was "Brothers in Arms." From their military postings around the nation and the world, the Barry brothers sent letters home that found their way into the popular newspaper column. Their frequent humor helped to lighten the ponderous material running on other pages.

Several selections from Mike Barry's contributions to the "Brothers in Arms" feature follow his father's brief assessment of the Holocaust.

Many historians have disputed how early the horror of the Jewish Holocaust under Hitler was generally known to the American public. As early as January 1943, editor John J. Barry presented what he termed a "horrible story."

The Jewish Massacre
January 23, 1943

The civilized world is horrified over the cruel treatment and persecution meted out to millions of defenseless Jews by Hitler, but few know the real extent of that persecution. The Jew was a tiny minority in Germany, a small minority in every European country, but was singled out by the arch-criminal Hitler to cover up his real schemes for power and conquest.

Of Germany's 200,000 Jews in 1930, all but 40,000 have

been deported or have perished; of Austria's 75,000, all but 15,000, at most; of the 80,000 in Bohemia and Moravia, all but 15,000. In Poland more than 600,000 have died. In Holland 60,000 remain out of 180,000; in Yugoslavia 96,000 out of 100,000 are dead, deported, or imprisoned; in Greece all between the ages of 18 and 45 have been enslaved, and an unknown number are dead.

In France 35,000 out of 300,000 have been deported; of Rumania's 900,000, all but 270,000 are imprisoned, enslaved, deported, or dead; Bulgaria has enslaved 8,500 out of 50,000; Slovakia has deported 70,000 out of 90,000; of Latvia's 100,000, one fourth are reported massacred, the others enslaved or starving in ghettos.

To sum up this horrible story, it is believed that 2,000,000 European Jews have perished and that 5,000,000 are in danger of extermination. This is the work of Adolf Hitler and his new order.

From the Pacific, Mike Barry reported on hearing the seventieth Kentucky Derby, which was won by Calumet Farm's Pensive.

The Seventieth Derby
May 20, 1944

This, too, is an historic date. I have just listened to the running of the seventieth derby, the third since our war began and the third I've missed in twenty-three years.

We have a public address system set up in our area, over which we broadcast official announcements, music, news, etc. I suggested to the officer in charge that we hook up a radio and carry the running of the classic.

"I don't know," he said, "Is it of general interest?"

He gets a military funeral Monday.

Our time is four and a half hours behind Louisville time, and both Hawaii stations carried the running from twelve-thirty to one o'clock. In the pool on the race I drew Gay Bit, and I'm still not sure he didn't win. The last I heard he was in a photo finish with Pensive and Gillette Blue Blades.

We had no choice other than to listen to Ted Husing. This was better than no broadcast at all, but not much better.

That's all, sister.

MIKE.

From the island of Oahu, Mike Barry recalled how in Louisville, in December 1941, he had heard the news of the Pearl Harbor attack.

Pearl Harbor Recalled

May 20, 1944

Oahu, May 6, 1944.

Dear Helen:

The afternoon of December 7, 1941, I was sitting in the living room listening to the regular Sunday concert of the Philharmonic. Our lowbrow brother, Tom, had his private radio tuned to a pro football game, when suddenly he yelled from the dining room "Hey Mike, the Japs are bombing Oahu!"

At that precise moment I should have made some historic remark, one that would have gone ringing down through the years. The bombing of Oahu meant the outbreak of war, shooting war, and just then it affected me more than any other member of the family. I was in the Enlisted Reserve Corps after four months of active duty, and subject to immediate recall.

Within twenty-four hours, I could be back in uniform and trudging down the paths of glory, which before had led but to the USO. Now it could mean something infinitely more serious, perhaps even a camp where there was no USO.

That was the call to arms Tom was sounding, but it left me unmoved. When he yelled "Hey Mike, the Japs are bombing Oahu!" my contribution to history's pages consisted of four words:

"The hell they are!"

* * *

You see, sister dear, I thought Tom was saying "Wahoo," and I didn't know where Wahoo was. Had I known he was saying Oahu it wouldn't have made any difference, because I didn't know where that was, either.

Now I know. I'm on Wahoo. Pardon me, Oahu.

I'd hate to tell you how long this war was going before I got straight in my mind the basic geography of the Pacific theatre. I was always getting Hawaii and the Philippines mixed up, and it was months before I could get Honolulu and Manila out of each other's suburbs.

Now, after years of constant study and a few sly peeks at the map on the wall beside me, I am equipped to swap small talk with either Rand, McNally or both.

Want a short refresher course? The Hawaiian Islands are some 2400 miles from our west coast, and some 3400 miles from Japan. These Islands consist of Hawaii, the largest, Oahu, the most populous, Molokai, the leper colony, and some others. The city of Honolulu is on Oahu. So is Pearl Harbor and Hickaam [Hickman] Field and Schofield Barracks, names you may remember.

And so am I.

* * *

A visit from movie star Betty Hutton and her USO troupe was vividly described.

The Terrific Betty Hutton

November 18, 1944

Now after seven months, I am happy to report there are some stars out this way, and we don't have to depend entirely on radio Tokyo for our entertainment.

Betty Hutton and her show just finished a 3-day stand

here. With a break in the weather, the engineers and the seabees hope to repair the damage in three weeks.

It's murder, she says, and she ain't foolin'. This doll is dynamite.

When she isn't tearing a microphone apart or making the faces only she can make, Betty is a good-looking girl. Of course the fact that she's blond didn't hurt her any in my handicap, either.

* * *

I wouldn't go broke betting those golden locks didn't come out of a bottle, but the peaches and cream complexion that went with 'em was really the skin I'd love to clutch, and it was all her own. Her hair-do was the halo variety, her dress a simple afternoon frock (I practically never miss an issue of Vogue) of brown with a narrow white notched lapel collar, and she wore shoes and stockings!

I've been looking at natives so long I didn't know girls wore those any more. Shoes and stockings, I mean.

Some of the fellows said later her stocking seams were twisted, but I wouldn't know. I never notice things like that.

* * *

The show was made up of usual trio—accordion, clarinet, guitar—an acrobatic dancer, a comic juggler, and Betty.

No grand built-up appearance for this young lady—she just walked out on the platform and started introducing the other acts. I liked the acrobatic dancer as well as I like acrobats, and I don't like acrobats, but either her art or her costume made a terrific hit with this GI audience. The comic juggler, an old vaudeville vet, was good. I know I saw him play in Louisville on the Keith circuit. I think the name was Val Betts or something like that.

Betty was terrific. She sang her theme song "Murder, he says," a sweet version of "It had to be you," then wrecked the joint with a new one called "Rockin' Horse." The encore was "Doin' It For Defense."

Believe me, she did it.

The formal surrender of the Japanese in September 1945 found Mike Barry in Tokyo commenting on General Douglas MacArthur.

The Japanese Surrender

September 29, 1945

Yokohama, 8 September '45

Dear Helen:

I'd say this has been quite a day. Drove to Tokyo this morning to see the formal entrance of American troops—the 1st Cavalry Division—and talked my way into the grounds of the United States Embassy, where General MacArthur presided at the raising of the Stars and Stripes.

Held in the beautiful garden, the ceremony was brief, and there were no spectators. Unless you count me. There was the honor squadron of the 7th Regiment, a few hundred correspondents and photographers, and assorted generals.

When the band played "The Star Spangled Banner," the flag was raised, and we stood there at present arms, I was a proud man. I knew I'd never be in a better place at a better time, or in better company.

* * *

The General was in grand form. That guy was born to be Supreme Commander of something

In rare good humor, too. He didn't get mad when I kept shouldering him aside trying to get in front of the newsreel cameramen. You know I hate publicity, but I figure if those fellows are determined to take my picture the least I can do is cooperate.

Yes, sir, Mac was quite pleasant. Even when I pushed him off balance so Fox Movietone could get a better shot at my profile, he merely turned and spoke to his chief of staff. In the pompous, majestic tones for which he's famous, he said, "Throw that bum out!"

* * *

In Tokyo, after the surrender, Barry heard strains of "My Old Kentucky Home." On this occasion he met Barry Bingham, editor of the Louisville *Courier-Journal*

My Old Kentucky Home—Tokyo Version
October 13, 1945

Yokohama, 15 Sept. '45

Dear Helen:

I was at a dinner last night in Tokyo, given by the Commander-in-chief for all the war correspondents, many of whom will be leaving shortly. Seems they've run out of war to cover.

Right away I want to make one thing clear—don't ask me how I got there, or how I've gotten to any of these places I've written about lately. If I had the slightest control over my movements I'd now be in Walgreen's, surrounded by huge malted milks, writing notes to Jim that he needn't worry about his 28 points—we'd have him outa there by Christmas. Of course I wouldn't say what Christmas, but he knows.

* * *

The dinner was preceded by two hours of determined drinking in the bar of the Dai-Iti Hotel, and when the scribes assembled in the dining room their mood can best be described as festive. I can't report on the whiskey, but there was an unlimited quantity of Jap beer. It comes in quart bottles and is reputed to be 16%.

Fortunately I don't like the taste. I shudder to contemplate the spectacle of an amateur 3.2 man trying to handle sweet sixteen. Last night I had one glass, and the only reason I didn't slap General MacArthur on the back was because he wasn't there. I understand he was scheduled to make a brief appearance, but when I left at 9:30 they were no longer expecting him.

It was probably just as well. I can't imagine the General in the midst of revelry any more than I could picture a boisterous bishop.

* * *

We had music by a Jap band, who looked strange with long hair. They played that kind of music, too, but then I'm an old square anyway and didn't mind at all. Don't know exactly what they played. It sounded like gypsy stuff, but who ever heard of a Japanese gypsy?

A little later on, inspired by I don't know what, this Far Eastern branch of the Hoosier Hot Shots gave out with "Dixie," producing wild rebel yells all over the joint. One correspondent, doubtless a Yankee, mistook the Confederate battle cry for an Indian war whoop and began dancing vigorously. We palefaces cheered him on.

* * *

Then came the payoff. They played "My Old Kentucky Home." I stood up and yelled, a performance which would have astounded any of my friends back home, you knowing what a quiet type I am at parties. To my amazement, I discovered I was the only Kentuckian present.

At least I was the only one on his feet. Then I saw Lieutenant Commander Barry Bingham sitting at a table across the room, deeply engrossed in conversation. I was certain he wasn't aware of what the band was valiantly attempting to play, so I went over.

"On your feet, Commander," I said, "or I'll blacken your name all over the state!" He didn't catch on. "Don't you hear what they're playing? That's 'My Old Kentucky Home'!"

"The hell it is!" said the commander, and immediately he was on his feet cheering for the home team. "Come on," he said, "we'll sing it!"

Whereupon Lieutenant Commander Barry Bingham, representing the United States Navy, the Courier-Journal, the Louisville Times, Radio Station WHAS and the better element, harmonized with Captain John Michael Barry, representing the Army Air Corps, the Kentucky Irish American, the 77th Infantry Division, the American Association, the Kentucky Jockey Club and the people in front of the scoreboard at Goodman's News Stand.

* * *

Modesty or no modesty, I must admit the applause was tremendous. This Bingham can sing almost as loud as I can, although naturally his voice lacks the professional finish of mine. So many, many people have said my voice is one of the most finished they've ever heard.

If anyone inquires, we are available at short notice for clubs or private parties. (This definitely does not mean private parties with clubs.) We have dress clothes, although our repertoire of Southern folk songs can be rendered most effectively in blackface. Yassuh!

A few slubs of that Jap beer wouldn't hurt the performance any, either.

* * *

During the pre-dinner drinking session, the Jap waitresses seemed to be having as much fun as anybody, but toward the close they were all huddled together having a good cry. Naturally I assumed some of the celebrants had gotten a little . . . uh, shall we say fresh?

Let's don't because we'd be wrong. The correspondents and officers had all been little gentlemen. It was just that the girls had learned the reason for the party.

It was a victory celebration.

MIKE.

2

The Cold War Over There

No sooner had Mike Barry assumed the role of editor of the *Irish American* in 1950 than the nation found itself again in a shooting war, this time in Korea. The United States had just learned in 1949 that the Soviet Union had a powerful nuclear capability, and apocalyptic fears tracked deeply into the national consciousness. Such specters frequently haunted the columns of the paper as well.

Korea, Cuba, Berlin, Vietnam, the Middle East, and nuclear proliferation—all were subjects for editorial commentary by Mike Barry. The editor's voice at the start of the Korean War could be harsh and bellicose. The careful reader will soon detect a shift in tone.

While Barry never became a pacifist, his response to the possibility of military conflict became increasingly measured and cautious. Especially chastened by the Cuban Missile Crisis in 1962, the *Irish American* editor began to speak of "cowards who want war, because they haven't the courage to live with danger."

A short and startling editorial in the first year of the Korean War called for dropping the atomic bomb.

Drop It Now
December 2, 1950

We think the question of whether or not to drop the atom bomb on those Chinese Communist forces is purely a military one. If it's practical, let's drop it immediately.

We don't see where there's any moral problem involved. If it's all right to kill the Reds one at a time with rifle bullets, by the dozens with artillery shells, or by the scores with thousand-pound aerial bombs, why is it morally wrong to kill them by the thousands with an atomic weapon?

It must be nice to be a GI these days in Korea. Enduring the unendurable in living conditions in immediate danger of being killed or maimed, while back home well-meaning civilians, eating hot food and sleeping in warm beds, say they're against using the atom bomb because "it just isn't right."

To kill a thousand Reds individually is all right. To kill a thousand at one time is all wrong. Why?

We didn't ask for this fight. Now that we're involved, let's go all the way.

One week later, the appeal for total engagement was resumed, though with a bow to "good reasons" why an atomic bomb might not be appropriate.

Brave People
December 9, 1950

There are probably a lot of good reasons why we shouldn't use the atom bomb on our enemies in Korea, but one you hear advanced quite often won't stand up under analysis.

It's this: We mustn't drop the bomb on the Communist forces, or the Russians are liable to start dropping them on this county.

In other words, it's all right for the GI's over in Korea to get the hell shot out of themselves, but we precious civilians here on the home front mustn't be exposed to any danger.

Why not? What makes our skins any more valuable than theirs?

There's only one kind of war in this modern world, and that's total war. Total war means we're all in it, and if we're going to be all in it together there's no reason why a few should be in over their heads, while the rest of us don't even get our feet wet.

The Christmas editorial of 1950 evoked the danger of a third world war.

Sad Christmas
December 23, 1950

We are coming up to a sad Christmas, because we are at war, and it is even sadder to think what future Christmases are going to be. While the actual fighting is confined to a small area, and may soon be over, the awful threat of another world war hangs over us.

Slowly but surely we are being dragged into it. The outbreak is only a question of time, and even if it holds off another year or two, we are still going to live in a state of tension. Our homes will be broken up with our sons and brothers and fathers going into the armed forces, our womenfolk into the factories.

No earthly power can stop this drift toward World War III. Treaties are meaningless, and appeals to reason are lost upon Communist rulers who believe only in force. If we are to be saved, only God can save us.

There is no peace on earth, no good will among men.

Six days into 1951, the editor suggested that President Truman could save everyone a lot of time by submitting a two-word State of the Union address.

Two Words
January 6, 1951

President Truman has been wasting a lot of time preparing his "State of the Union" message to Congress, scheduled for delivery this coming Monday. He could cut the whole thing down to this: "It's lousy."

We have floundered from one mess into another for a long time, but now we seem to have gotten ourselves into the biggest one of all. As sure as shooting there's going to be shooting, and while we're trying to get ready with our usual frantic haste, the time is mighty short.

The first time it was the "war to end war." The one coming up looks like the "war to end everybody."

In World War II we had strong allies, who held the opposition on the five-yard-line while we argued whether or not freshmen were eligible for the varsity. Now the friends we have aren't very strong, and instead of trying to build them up a lot of us are saying we ought to throw 'em to the wolves and go along on our own.

Whether we're strong enough to do this single-handed is another question. For one thing, we sure as heck aren't united. Last time, everybody knew we had to whip the Germans and the Japs, and once the shooting started we were all one, big scrappy family.

Now there's plenty of shooting over in Korea, but are we united at home? Not by a long shot. A lot of us are saying we shouldn't have been in Korea in the first place. Others insist we ought to admit we're licked and get the hell out of there. There are plenty of us who keep saying if we pull out of Korea we'll have to pull out of Japan, then Okinawa, then the Philippines, and where do we stop? We'll have to be the ones who stop—it's a cinch the other guys won't.

As Republican Senator Henry Cabot Lodge of Massachusetts said last week, "I don't want to stand on the Himalayas, nor do I want to fight on Cape Cod."

And, while most of us are united on the fact that we're in danger, we have different ideas on what to do about it. Some want to start dropping atom bombs on Moscow right away. Others want to hide under the bed and wait for the storm to blow over.

The main concern of most of us is to "get in on the gravy" this time. We all want one of those big-pay, little-work war plant jobs. Those of us who were in the armed forces last time, with soft spots, are trying to find an even softer spot for the next one.

Oh, we're in great shape. The Democrats are split, the Republicans are split, the Armed Forces are split.

Asked to choose between guns and butter, our people are screaming "We want both!" And the butter had better not be oleo, either.

Everybody wants more money, lower prices, a bigger

army, less taxes, free enterprise, government support, and an egg in their beer.

President Truman doesn't have to tell us what the state of the Union is. We know.

The sixth anniversary of the death of President Franklin D. Roosevelt brought forth not only a review of the world in the first six postwar years, but also a paean to FDR.

Six Crowded Years
April 14, 1951

In all the hullabaloo over the firing of MacArthur on Wednesday, only a comparative handful of people remembered Thursday that it was the sixth anniversary of Roosevelt's death. And, even if the crisis hadn't been precipitated, its doubtful that many more would have remembered.

We are forgetting fast, not only Roosevelt but everything else. This is a fantastic age. There has simply been too much in the last twenty years for our poor human brains to understand. We went from a boom into a deadly depression, then only a brief space before we were plunged into war, climaxed by the atom bomb. Before we could reconvert to a peacetime economy, the rise of Communism all over the world forced us to rearm, and now we are engaged in a bitter war which at any moment may explode into World War III.

It's really hard to believe Roosevelt has been dead only six years. It seems much longer. Now we can realize why historians must wait years and years, so that they may look back on great events and view them in the proper perspective.

Surely it's too soon to judge the man who was President longer than anyone in our history. Right now there are too many people who think he was a scoundrel and too many who believe him a saint. The truth is somewhere in between.

Roosevelt had courage and optimism when we needed it so badly back in 1933, and he had the vision to foresee what was happening in Europe and to prepare us for it. Had an isolationist been elected in 1940, a man who would have tried to draw this country into a shell and allowed the dictators to go unchallenged, the history of the world would have been changed. It is almost a certainty that the Nazis would have conquered Europe, and Japan all of Asia. We would be fighting today, without a single ally, and against overwhelming odds—or we would have been beaten.

Those who hated Roosevelt before, and hate his memory now, claim he sold out to Russia. Perhaps he could have made better deals, if he could have known then what his critics know now, but then we were in the middle of a war, Russia was our ally, and any agreement with an ally that promised to save American lives seemed to be a good one.

The verdict will have to be left to history. But, with all his faults, there are many of us who will always believe that Americans, and lovers of freedom all over the world, should thank God for sending us Franklin Delano Roosevelt.

Written in the middle of the week of the Cuban Missile Crisis in October 1962, this editorial revealed the grimness of the national and local mood.

Only Halfway
October 27, 1962

When the fall race meeting opened Wednesday afternoon at Churchill Downs, two men watched a fellow they both knew shoving money every race through the $50 win window.

"Look at that Jake!" one of the men said. "He bets like there's no tomorrow."

"I know," said the other man, "but suppose he's right?"

So far, fortunately, Jake hasn't been right. The tomorrows are still creeping along in their petty pace and the last syllable of time has not yet been recorded.

But the clear and present danger is still clearly present. The man who says we have nothing to fear is a fool, because we are not dealing with logical, sensible, reasonable men. We are menaced by maniacs.

It's easy to say, and to believe, that the Russians aren't about to fight for Cuba, or bleed for Cuba, or die for Cuba. We all know the Russians don't give a damn for Cuba.

But who among us can sleep peacefully knowing that some of Castro's wild men have access to missiles aimed at this country?

Setting up the blockade is a perilous but necessary act. But it's only half the job, and by far the easier half. Surely we cannot allow the Cubans to possess offensive missiles, and the means to launch them. Therefore the bases must be dismantled by the Cubans themselves, either under U.N. supervision or ours, or we must use force to destroy them.

That the Cubans—or Russians—would do the job themselves seems too much to hope for. Such abject surrender would mean a loss of face intolerable to Khrushchev, and the absolute end for Castro.

We seem to be left with the alternative, grim as it must be. Nor can there be the slightest doubt that President Kennedy will not hesitate to use force—when it is necessary.

The week after the height of the crisis had passed, editor Barry suggested that the nation had survived "by the skin of our teeth."

Skin Thin

November 3, 1962

Maybe we've got a chance. Thornton Wilder's famous play "The Skin of Our Teeth," you will recall, depicted how man from the beginning of time had survived innumerable perils—prehistoric monsters, flood, fire, famine, war. "The whole bit," as survivors now around to prove Wilder was right like to say.

Just a week ago we were within a button-push of destruction. The Good Lord said "Not yet," the miracle of the Russians' backing down resulted, and so we're still here.

That's why we're optimistic. Having squeezed through so many tight places, it's even possible we'll survive the peril that awaits us next Tuesday—Election Day.

But don't get overconfident. And keep your fallout shelter well stocked. It could come in handy even if we do get through The Longest Day of November 6, because nobody knows how fast we'll get back to that international game called "Anyone For Oblivion?"

At this writing things on the world front are going better than anybody would have dared hope a week ago. Castro's stubbornness shouldn't surprise you, and certainly shouldn't worry you. Without Russian help, what can he do to us? Just as MacArthur bypassed Jap-held islands in the Pacific, Cuba can now be isolated and the Castro regime allowed to collapse of its own weaknesses.

Once the Russian offensive weapons are out of Cuba, we'll have nothing to worry about.

Nothing except Berlin, Laos, Vietnam . . .

The next time the Russians show their muscle, you can be sure it'll be a lot closer to home. It will be a place where all the conditions favor them. Luckily for us, and for the rest of the world, we had the big edge in Cuba.

We're not likely to have such an edge anywhere else, but then next time we won't have to worry about President Kennedy making any foolish mistakes.

What's that? You thought he did pretty well? Goodness, you've naive. Don't you know Eddie Rickenbacker and some of his fellow squirrels have had to form another committee to save us from Kennedy?

They call this one the "Committee for the Monroe Doctrine," which is a real peachy title. Once the committee gets the clock turned back about a century and a half, so that conditions will be just as they were when Jimmy Monroe dashed off that gold star composition, Eddie and the other members can clear up a few little details.

It seems that Monroe, when he suggested rather firmly that European nations stay out of our backyard, also pledged that we couldn't let our kids run across their lawns. Therefore if we want everybody to live up to the Monroe Doctrine, we'll have to set the good example by bringing back to this country all soldiers, military advisors, weapons and everything else now stationed abroad.

Naturally this would include missiles from Turkey.

If you think this may present a few problems, don't worry. Rickenbacker and committee will provide the answers.

We said it before and we'll say it again. Eddie was out on that raft too long.

National debate over President John F. Kennedy's Nuclear Non-Proliferation Treaty brought forward the implied plea to have the courage to live with danger.

Cowards for War
March 2, 1963

There must be times when John Fitzgerald Kennedy wishes he were like so many other sons of rich fathers; one of the playboys whose life is devoted to golf, gals, sports cars and night clubs, whose toughest decision is whether to go skiing or sunning.

It's an existence he could have chosen, as could his brothers. And Nelson Rockefeller, and a few others.

Right now could be one of the times. The President's popularity still ranks high with the people, but the word doesn't seem to have reached Washington. There he seems to be opposed by everybody in Congress.

On the home front, Kennedy's tax proposals are getting nowhere. He's going to try to shove through Medicare again, once more against formidable opposition. His ideas of Federal aid to education are smothered by a fight over Adam Clayton Powell's peculiar peregrinations.

The President's got labor troubles like you never saw. When he quite properly singled out the printers' union boss,

Bert Powers, as the biggest obstacle to settlement of the disastrous New York newspaper strike, Powers contemptuously brushed it aside with, "The President is ill-advised."

The President's brother is still battling Jimmy Hoffa on all fronts and has a clean slate on every one—he hasn't won any.

But it's in foreign affairs where the President has the biggest headaches. He has problems he didn't make, problems nobody before him ever solved, problems he will most assuredly leave to his successor—for there are no answers.

Kennedy's main concern is to preserve the United States and world peace. The two cannot be separated, a fact so basic it is incredible how many Americans can't see it.

The President's worst troubles come from these people. They are the cowards who want war, because they haven't the courage to live with danger.

"It is nothing short of tragic," the St. Louis Post Dispatch said last week, "that the country is being deluged with irresponsible propaganda designed to destroy confidence in United States foreign policy, particularly with respect to Cuba.

"If the Cuban problem can be solved at all it can be solved only with patience, steady nerves and a policy based coldly on the facts as they are. But opponents keep on frustrating the formulation of a sane policy, and if they keep it up they can cause untold harm."

Isn't it obvious they have already caused untold harm? Their continuing outcry for an invasion of Cuba has practically forced Khrushchev to stiffen his attitude. Whether the Red dictator believes an invasion is likely or no, he dare not crawl. He's got to stand up in front of his people wearing a uniform and proclaim Russia's readiness for war. Khrushchev has got to think of Nikita—if he shows weakness he'll be out.

Khrushchev knows Kennedy—after last October he certainly should. But he also knows our Congress is liberally sprinkled with hotheads who'd vote for war in a minute.

Under the circumstances, how can Kennedy possibly negotiate with Khrushchev on a nuclear test ban, on Berlin, or on anything?

When you ask this question, you get a quick reply: "Don't negotiate with them at all! You can't trust those dirty Reds!"

Very well, no negotiations. We'll just keep building bigger bombs, and testing bigger bombs, and the Russians will keep building bigger bombs than ours, and testing bigger bombs, and the French will test bigger bombs, and the Red Chinese will test bombs . . .

The St. Patrick's Day edition of 1963 featured yet another satirical report on the state of the nation.

Free From Care
March 16, 1963

Grand indeed it is that St. Patrick's Day should find us all so happy and carefree, with no problems. None at all.

No money problem. With credit unlimited and deficit financing the fashion, who worries about money?

No peace problem. Why, we've got so much peace there's a surplus. People are getting bored, restless. They're not coming right out and saying they want war, but they keep coming up with ideas that will get rid of this peace surplus pretty doggone quick.

No labor problem. Workers keep asking for shorter hours and more money, and those who don't get 'em get vacations—on the picket line. The nation's railroads are getting ready to give thousands of obsolete firemen the whole summer off. And the fall. And the winter. And next summer.

No domestic problem. Taxes are going to be cut, government benefits are going up. Every branch of government has the same wonderful idea—take less from the people and give back more. It's just a question of time before the only guys that will have to work will be the letter carriers. Sure and you wouldn't want to use up any of your precious leisure time going after your government check, would you now?

The angels did a lot for Ireland, sprinkling the land with star dust and dotting it with silver, and St. Patrick drove out the snakes and finally they got rid of the English, but still the Irish of a few generations ago showed a lot of foresight in leaving that blessed land to come to America.

They thought it would be better for their children, and their children's children, and they were right. America was a grand country.

But it sure couldn't compare with what we have now—Utopia.

By the time of the American involvement in Vietnam, Mike Barry was both sparing and cautious in his commentary on what course the nation should follow. He lauded President Lyndon Johnson's "bombing pause" of March 31, 1968.

Light Ahead
April 6, 1968

Not quite two hundred years ago some embattled farmers fired the shot that was heard 'round the world. The speed of sound was just as fast in those days, but not the speed of communications, so news of the rustic revolt was slow in spreading to the far corners.

We live in the electronic age, when communication is almost instant. President Johnson fired his shot Sunday night, and it was heard 'round the world before the hour was up.

And the echoes are still ringing. This is not surprising, because it was history in the making. Live history, right before our eyes and ears; words that would affect the lives of all of us.

Words, in fact, that could save the lives of many of our young men. It has become more painfully clear all the time that the men in Hanoi were determined not to negotiate with Lyndon Johnson. The President tried every way he knew, every possible avenue of approach—the UN, our friends in other countries, our enemies in other countries, neutrals, the Pope—and never once did Hanoi respond.

Of course it is possible the enemy won't negotiate with Johnson's successor, but we don't know. We do know they won't talk to LBJ. Now there is a chance, a hope.

At last there is light at the end of the dark tunnel.

In the midst of the troubled summer of 1968, the *Irish American* called the Vietnam War one that "nobody wants and nobody can figure a way to get out of." The subheading of the editorial read: "All You Need for Restful Summer Is Lobotomy."

Onward and Downward
July 20, 1968

The whole world made progress this week, but only on its way to hell in a handbasket. Otherwise, all things stayed just about the same except for the places where they got worse.

We are still up to here in Vietnam, a war nobody wants and nobody can figure a way to get out of. Here at home the people involved in our domestic problems keep making the problems bigger instead of helping with the solutions, our government officials on every level are frantically trying to meet rising prices with fixed revenues, and our two major parties seem about to nominate the two candidates the people don't want to be President.

There's nothing like a quiet, peaceful, carefree summer. That's what this one is nothing like.

We're not even going to get a vacation from Congress. Both Houses will recess long enough for the two national conventions in August, then go back to what is loosely referred to as their legislative duties after Labor Day.

Anyone for a cold one?

3

The Cold War at Home

The cold war years were not just a time of frazzled nerves for Americans who feared the nuclear might of a Communist enemy without. Alongside this international tension Americans felt the anxiety of the suspicion of subversion and treason on the American home front.

Worldwide Catholicism had a particularly high anti-Communist animus, especially within the pontificate of the rigidly orthodox Pius XII, who served as pope from 1939 to 1958. America's leading anti-Communist crusader was also a Catholic, Senator Joseph R. McCarthy (1908-57) of Wisconsin. While such national Catholic periodicals as *America* and *Commonweal* challenged the Wisconsin senator long before his censure by the U.S. Senate in December 1954, Irish Catholic Mike Barry became an early and vocal critic of McCarthy in the pages of the *Irish American*. After the senator's fall, Barry made his next major target the excessive patriots in the ranks of the John Birch Society, particularly in the person of a clerical Birch supporter, Fr. Richard Ginder.

As early as November 1952, the *Irish American* referred to Senator McCarthy's accusations about Communists in high places in American life as "fantastic lies."

One Man Team
November 8, 1952

A City Hall official walked into Democratic headquarters about 6 o'clock Tuesday evening and asked John Crimmins [Jefferson County Democratic party chairman] how things were going.

"We're about twelve thousand behind," said Johnny, "and losing ground."

"Good heavens!" cried the official. "We've run out of poor people!"

We're pretty sure he was joking, but he was expressing the thought of a lot of Democrats who believe the people have been prosperous so long they've forgotten hard times. These Democrats are a little bitter, feeling the voters are an ungrateful lot.

They just couldn't be wronger. Prosperity—if you want to call deficit financing that—was a minor issue last Tuesday. A major issue was war, the war we're fighting now and the big war we're getting ready to fight. Another major issue, particularly to the Catholic voters, was Communists in government.

If these Catholics had stopped to think, they might have realized that the Truman administration, instead of being sympathetic toward Communists, had fought them in every part of the world where a fight was possible. Had the Republicans in Congress been successful in their fight against all forms of foreign aid, both economic and military, the Russians would now be a lot farther along on their road to world conquest.

But Catholics by the thousands swallowed McCarthy's fantastic lies. In their eagerness to believe the Wisconsin faker, they even turned against their own Catholic papers. They wrote angry letters to official diocesan papers which had criticized McCarthy.

Here in Louisville "The Record," official publication of the archdiocese, had a thoughtful editorial headed "McCarthyism in Perspective" in its October 24 issue.

Its letters-to-the-editor column a week later, October 31, was revealing. One writer said the only explanation for a Catholic's failure to believe McCarthy was "intellectual dishonesty or organic mental illness."

The editor of The Record replied that the editorial "was directed at McCarthy. It was not directed at the Republican Party, much less at all Republican candidates."

This explanation, and all other attempts to persuade

Catholics to examine McCarthy's record more closely, were useless.

When baseball's Cincinnati Reds took to calling themselves the "Redlegs" because their traditional title might sound subversive, editor and sportsman Barry had clearly had enough.

We Surrender Another Word

April 18, 1953

Several weeks ago we reprinted John Steinbeck's wonderful piece, "The King Snake and the Rattlers," a parable for Americans. The noted novelist pointed out we are so afraid of the Communists that we are surrendering some of our dearest possessions, our most meaningful words.

"It's about time we began fighting for our words!" wrote Steinbeck. "The Communists have conquered some of our most holy words simply by using them and getting them dirty. Instead of taking them back and washing them off, we have haughtily walked away from such words . . ."

Just this week the sports pages of our papers carried the news of another surrender. "In the future," said the notice, "the management of the Cincinnati Baseball Club requests that the team be referred to as 'the Redlegs' instead of 'the Reds.' "

Fourteen years ago the pennant winners of the National League were the Cincinnati Reds, and thirteen years ago the champions of the entire baseball world were the Cincinnati Reds. Both times it was the Reds, not the Redlegs.

It's an old and honored name in baseball, the Reds. As the closest major league team to Louisville, the Reds have always been our "second home team."

Now we have to stop calling the Cincinnati team the Reds. We're supposed to say they're Redlegs.

Why?

Obviously because the club management feels "the Reds" makes too many people think of our Communist enemies.

Their feelings are entirely too sensitive. When we think of anything connected with baseball, we think of the United States of America, where it's the national game, where even the President was criticized for neglecting the tradition of throwing out the first ball.

"It is time to retake our words," wrote Steinbeck, "and polish them up to their former brightness and live by them, instead of abandoning them and denying them and pretending we never heard of them. We must recapture our words."

We are making a poor start, Mr. Steinbeck. If this Redleg business is a sample, we are just surrendering more.

Holy Week 1961 found the tolerance of editor Barry stretched to the limits once again.

Sweeter Still
April 1, 1961

This being Holy Week, it is perhaps appropriate that this department of sweetness and light, dripping with charity and with only an occasional mild reproach written more in sorrow than in anger, be kinder than usual.

Therefore we are not going to comment on the report from Washington that Kentucky ranks 21st in population density, lest something slip out about how dense they were in '55 and how much denser they're likely to be in '63. This is not the time.

Nor will we mention Father Ginder and the note in Our Sunday Visitor saying his name is pronounced with a soft "g," lest we burst forth with "How appropriate! Matches his head!"

We intend to ignore the many letters-to-the-editor in local papers from the lunatic fringe, all supporting the John Birch Society's ideals and blindly endorsing the Un-American activities of the House Un-American Activities Committee. We will bear in mind it takes all kinds of people to make a world, even if this isn't the kind of world we're trying to make.

None of this now. Maybe later, but not now.

Cardinal Richard Cushing of Boston aroused the editor's ire and evoked the delicate suggestion that His Eminence should (piously) shut up.

The Lip, Ecclesiastical Version
May 2, 1964

If you have visitors from Boston, try reversing the field and asking them questions. For instance, what gives with Cardinal Cushing?

Branch Rickey once described Leo Durocher as a man who could walk into an impossible situation and immediately make it worse.

The cardinal gave a great exhibition of this last week with his revolving door statements on the Birchers. He said he was sorry he had ever indorsed them and he was long overdue in withdrawing his indorsement.

A few days later, wedging his red-slippered foot back into his big mouth, Cardinal Cushing said he had been misinformed. The Birchers hadn't really said all the terrible things someone had told him they'd said.

Too bad he isn't a Trappist. They have a vow of silence.

Robert Welch, leader of the John Birch Society, came in for especially strong fire in the summer of 1964, a season that had seen conservative Republican Barry Goldwater nominated for the presidency.

One Only
August 15, 1964

Robert Welch, der fuehrer of der Birchers, got long and loud applause from a bunch of Communists last week. His audience of 600, the news story said, gave Welch a standing ovation when he finished a two-hour speech.

It's possible, of course, the listeners were simply expressing their joy that Welch' marathon talk was over. Two hours! Was he going after Castro's record?

While the affair was billed as the annual convention of the Christian Crusade, it's definite Welch's audience of 600 were all Communists. They had to be.

They obviously weren't all Robert Welch, and anybody who isn't Robert Welch is a dirty Red. If you doubt this, you Commie you, go read Welch's writings.

Robert will convince you that you might as well be a Communist—it's the only way you can get along in this Commie country.

If you're looking for justice, for instance, your party card would be a big help. Welch has written: "We must face the fact that our courts have by no means been immune to Communist infiltration."

Need medical treatment? Avoid that long wait in the doctor's office or the wrong medicine—show 'em you're a Red. "The American Medical Association," Welch wrote, "has now been 'took' to the extent that we could not count on any direct help there."

Want to work for civil rights? Okay, but before you ship out, shape up. "The trouble in our Southern states," says the one-man country's only American, "has been fomented almost entirely by Communists."

You really can't enjoy reading a paper, watching TV or listening to the radio unless you're with it. According to Welch, "the domination of our press, television and radio by Communist influences is now so great that you simply are not allowed to learn or be reminded of the real nature of the beasts to whom we are losing." (And don't you want to get on the winning side?)

Looking for spiritual comfort? "Fully one third of the services in the Protestant churches are helping the breakdown of fundamentalist religion. Some ministers actually use their pulpits to preach outright communism, often in very thin disguise if any, while having the hypocrisy to thank God in public for their progressive apostasy."

Also Commies have infiltrated the Catholic priesthood—Welch's estimated figure is "one-half of 1%."

If you're interested in a political career, either as a Democrat or a Republican you'd better line up with the top men. Welch says President Roosevelt "was guilty of plain unadulterated treason." He's a little more charitable with President Eisenhower, saying he was either a tool of the Communists or too stupid to know what they were doing. All Ike admirers will thus be glad to know Welch gives them a choice—the former President was either a traitor or an idiot.

"Or, to put the matter bluntly," Welch wrote of Eisenhower, "he has been sympathetic to Communist aims, realistically and even mercilessly willing to help them achieve their goals, knowingly receiving and abiding by Communist orders, and consciously serving the Communist conspiracy, for all of his adult life."

But don't think FDR started it all. According to Welch, our first Communist president was Woodrow Wilson—"It is hard to tell how much of the tragic disaster of those years was due to the conscious support of Communist purposes." (And all the time we thought our first Red leader was George Washington!)

Anyway, in addressing the 600 Communists in Dallas, Welch said that his Birch Society "had been incredibly smeared." The leader said the Birchers are "a permanent and growing body." Like a malignant tumor?

On October 4, 1965, Pope Paul VI (1963-78) had addressed the United Nations in New York. Here the Catholic editor found fresh ammunition against those of his fellow Catholics who thought the United Nations a dangerous force.

Catholic Rightists Most Violent
October 9, 1965

On the righthand side of this page there is reprinted an editorial from The St. Louis Post-Dispatch commenting on the Pope's visit to the United Nations. In it the paper suggests that the isolationists and conservatives who have been attacking the UN should now reconsider.

The Post-Dispatch said this applies to some American Catholics "and specifically to a few Catholic groups in St. Louis." (This was in reference to one extremist bunch calling themselves a chapter of the Cardinal Mindzenty group or foundation or somesuch.)

Wrote the Post-Dispatch:

"Those who respect the Pope must now, we should think, respect the UN."

Of course they should, but will they? Not likely.

The Catholic members of these nut outfits are real gone kooks, violent in their extremism. Look at all the priests who are members of the Birch Society. When Father Ginder, a member of the national board of the Birchnuts, had to stop writing his vicious nonsense in "Our Sunday Visitor" on account of what was charitably described as mental and physical exhaustion, he was succeeded by Father Coogan, who's just as bad. Not many priests in the Louisville archdiocese agree with these knuckleheads, but the weekly containing their dangerous trash is still distributed at church doors here.

A couple of years ago the weekly "America," published by the Jesuit fathers, ran an article sharply critical of the Birch Society. Immediately the magazine was swamped with letters—some from priests—insisting that the Communists had taken over the Jesuit order.

We have long felt that what makes so many Catholics pushovers for every rightist movement is the one added word—either "atheistic" or "godless." No speaker or writer for the nut groups ever says his bunch is fighting Communism—it's always "atheist Communism" or "godless Communism."

Man, does this get 'em! Right away they're crusaders of old. Start yelling "God wills it!" and you could get a boatload willing to go over and charge the Kremlin walls.

You'd think that nowhere in this blessed land was there ever any atheistic capitalism or godless capitalism.

Now let the Catholic Birchers note that Pope Paul called his address to the United Nations "a solemn ratification of this lofty institution." The UN, the Holy Father added, must never fail—"Let unanimous trust in this institution grow, let its authority increase . . ."

"Is there anyone," the Pope asked, "who does not see the necessity of coming thus progressively to the establishment of a world authority?"

The sad truth is there is, and more than one.

But no more can Catholic members of extremist groups rattle off their muddled version of some old encyclical to uphold their views. Pope Paul VI has made it crystal clear that he believes in the UN as the world's best hope for peace, that he supports the UN with all his heart.

Catholics do not have to agree with the Pope, this not being a matter of faith or morals, but his appearance at the UN and his strongly expressed approval should at least make some of them take a second look at the rightist fronts they've been supporting.

Also, the Pope's address should cut down the number of wild outcries that "The Communists have taken over the Vatican!"

Please note we suggest a reduction. It would be foolish to expect a complete elimination.

Although the *Irish American* applauded the moderate civil rights movement of the 1960s, it was not about to write a blanket endorsement for that decade's youth culture.

The Military Mind in Action

June 8, 1968

General James M. Gavin, author of "Crisis Now," told the booksellers convention in Washington this week that student disorders stemmed from the fact that "colleges and universities have become more and more remote from those they are intended to serve, and people today know more about everything in the world than the heads of state did a generation ago."

The General was applauded when he said he favored voting privileges for 18-year-olds—"If they're old enough to die, they're old enough to vote."

Exactly. Naturally we all hope they don't have to prove one to do the other.

But General Gavin's concluding remarks, which were applauded, are certainly open to argument:

"In my opinion this is the finest generation we've ever had in this country. They're dedicated, committed, hard-working, and darned tired of being frustrated by all the double talk about what must get done and doesn't get done."

That may be the General's opinion. Those of us who lived through the depression, then World War II, then the struggle to readjust and find a job and a place to live and to raise a family, plus all of the deliriously happy times of the past few years of riots and revolts, sometimes feel the present generation hasn't the slightest idea of how hard and brutal and difficult life can be.

They never had it so good, and yet all they do is complain because it isn't better.

General, go blow it out your barracks bag.

4

The National Political Scene

Despite the fact that Mike Barry could readily fill lengthy columns year-round with what he often considered the calamitous foibles of Kentucky politics, he considered the national political scene his editorial beat as well. Not surprisingly, the *Irish American* remained staunchly loyal to its nineteenth-century Democratic roots throughout the Cold War years.

If there is a major surprise for latter-day historians in the post war columns, it is in Barry's somewhat late and somewhat reluctant support of fellow Irishman John F. Kennedy for the presidency. (Selections from columns on the Kennedys follow in Section 6) More predictable would be the figures on whom Barry trained his linguistic rifle barrels: Dwight D. Eisenhower, Barry Goldwater, J. Edgar Hoover, Joseph McCarthy, Richard Nixon, Ronald Reagan, and George Wallace.

"These are the times that try men's souls," . . . wrote Mike Barry immediately after the 1952 presidential election. The prospect of Richard Nixon as vice-president especially troubled the editor.

Pray We Must
November 22, 1952

If you have prayers, prepare to say them now. Our newly-elected President is getting ready to visit the promised land of Korea, just as he promised. The road is long and the perils are many, so let us pray.

Both Eisenhower and our country are in danger, the new President from the ordinary hazards of travel and the extraordinary hazards of visiting a combat zone, and our country from Ike's lawful successor.

These are the times that try men's souls, and the soul of

Richard Nixon so far exhibited to mortal judgment has been found wanting. The California Crier isn't made of the stern stuff we so desperately need.

He's a fake, a man who pretends to be something he isn't. Nixon got the vice presidential nomination in Chicago by modestly displaying his assets, but was careful to conceal the liabilities that would have instantly removed him from consideration.

Think back to that Chicago convention for a minute. Once Eisenhower was nominated, everything else was anti-climactic. The Republican delegates could have named John Doe or Richard Roe—in September a lot of them wished they had Richard Roe instead of Richard Nixon—and it wouldn't have changed the result in a single precinct.

If Nixon had been man enough to tell Republican leaders about his lovable group of sponsors, who were keeping him in a style to which a lot of us would like to become accustomed, he would have been passed up quicker than a drum majorette with bow legs. The No. 2 spot would have gone to any one of a dozen others, because it didn't make the slightest difference.

All the Republicans knew they needed was someone to fill out the ticket. Ike was going to do the running—the people would either vote for or against the No. 1 man.

When the storm broke in September over Nixon's private fund of $18,000, Dickie Boy first tried to brazen it out and then resorted to tears. A shoplifter caught for the first time uses exactly the same strategy, threatening to have the store detective fired when he grabs her and then bursting into sobs in the privacy of the manager's office.

To some of us who keep wanting to believe the American people as a whole are fairly intelligent, the ensuing reaction to Nixon's maudlin exhibition on a TV network was plumb discouraging. From coast to coast soft-hearted women and soft-headed men cried right along with him. Just a poor, misunderstood boy!

The bum might still be misunderstood, but he sure isn't

poor. Dickie Boy will pull down $30,000 a year and $10,000 more for expenses as Vice President, plus a Cadillac town car and chauffeur, two offices, more than $80,000 a year for office help and generous funds for telephone and telegraph bills.

It'll be interesting to see how he does on real estate now. If Senator Nixon could buy a $13,000 home in California and a $41,000 place in Washington, Vice President Nixon ought to be able to swing a deal for the Empire State Building.

Anyway, this is the sort of man who may suddenly be called upon to lead us through the awful days which most surely lie ahead, a man who twists the truth in little things like his wife's name and date of birth, who challenges his opponents to tell all and then tells only half himself, a man who uses a woman's defense—tears.

Verily, it is a time for prayer.

With television broadcasting only five years old in the area, Barry urged readers to get a set so they could watch the big show of the Eisenhower-Nixon inauguration. In his editorial, the editor managed to blast General MacArthur and Senator McCarthy as well.

Big Show

January 10, 1953

If you've been putting off buying a television set, preferring to squander your surplus cash on food, rent, clothes, doctor bills and other such nonsense, don't delay any longer than a week from next Tuesday. That'll be January 20, Inauguration Day.

The whole show's going to be televised, five big hours of it, and when you hear what the committee has planned you won't want to miss a single minute. Might be a good idea, in fact, to fix up a mess of sandwiches and coffee so you won't have to tear yourself away even for meals.

While there has been no formal announcement of many planned features, an unusually unreliable source in Washington has forwarded us the incredible details. Gosh, this TV show's going to have everything!

What do you look for in television—comedy, drama, excitement, love interest, intrigue, pathos, suspense?

The inaugural show will have them all!

You'll be knocked right off your living room sofa, for instance, right at the very beginning. The grand marshal of the parade—regardless of what you have heard before—will be General Douglas MacArthur, and when the Great I Am makes his first appearance he'll shatter picture tubes from Presque Isle to Pebble Beach.

Mac will wade ashore from a landing craft in the Potomac River. He'll be alone and unarmed, wearing that battered hat and smoking the ever-lovin' corncob, and nobody will come ashore ahead of him.

Nobody, that is, except two Army divisions, an extra regiment for clearance of snipers, and a 400-man honor guard. Mac will be on his own, although his path will have been cleared a little by a six-hour naval bombardment and there'll be several squadrons of jet fighters overhead.

While your nerves are still quivering, the cameras will immediately shift back to the peace and quiet of a studio. There, in the chaste simplicity of paneled walls, Vice President Nixon will re-enact his memorable television performance of the recent campaign. Just as he could in the privacy of the studio that night, with only his wife, his dog, several dozen assorted technicians, directors and scriptwriters looking on, you can give way to tears in your own living room.

A good cry will help you a lot. If the tears won't come readily, just think of the creep who'll spend the next four years in the high office of Vice President, just a heartbeat away from the Presidency. If that won't make you cry, you've got a heart of stone—and a head to match.

But you won't sit there sobbing for long. In a twinkling you'll be whisked back to Washington, where the parade is going full-force.

This will be the most amazing parade in history, on or off television. Made up of both Eisenhower and Taft supporters, it will go marching off in different directions at the same time!

In a separate division all by himself, you'll see "Fighting Joe" McCarthy. At first you'll think it strange to see him pushing a wheelbarrow, and you may blurt out, "Isn't that beneath the dignity of a United States Senator?" Then one of the literate members of your family will explain the fellow you're watching is McCarthy of Wisconsin, and that nothing is beneath his dignity.

But perhaps you're still puzzled, so you ask, "Why the wheelbarrow?"

"To carry his medals, you dope!" you'll be told.

Dumb as you are, you may wonder how a guy who RESIGNED from the Marines eight months before the war ended because he was refused a four-month leave to run for office, and who was a rear-echelon commando while in the service, could rate so many medals.

It will be explained to you that, according to the official records of the Marine Corps, McCarthy didn't rate any decorations. He got them because he applied for the medals, sending along certified copies of HIS OWN RECORDS to substantiate his claims.

At this point, it's best you quiet down. One unkind remark about Hero McCarthy and your own family will denounce you as a Communist, as it is well known this fearless defender of the faith is opposed only by Reds and Red-thinkers.

Besides, you'll want to get back to the TV screen. The floats are beginning to come by, and some of them are elaborate beyond words. One will show ex-President Truman playing the piano in a Western dance hall where General Vaughan's the bartender, another will depict Margaret Truman's future appearance on television—she's getting hit in the face by a succession of custard pies (after that Berle show last Tuesday night this will be considered a promotion), and a large float will show Senator McCarran defying Christopher Columbus to discover America until he's checked by the FBI and takes a loyalty oath.

There'll be laughs when the Puerto Rican delegate demands a poll of his delegation, love interest when Senator Taft sings of his undying love for Senator Taft, and wild cheers from the landlords of America as a coffin labeled "Rent Control" goes by.

Oh, it'll be a show you'll never forget. Don't miss it if you can.

With the same tone as his "promo" for the broadcast of the inaugural parade, Barry analysed the first month of Eisenhower's presidency.

Happy Day
February 14, 1953

Next week President Eisenhower will finish his first month in office, and what a happy land we now have! The war in Korea has been stopped, taxes have been cut, labor and management are in each other's arms, the farmers are screaming with joy, and city dwellers have never had it so good.

That's the way things are, and don't believe all the guff you read in the newspapers. It's all just a lot of lying Democratic propaganda.

What's going on in Korea is just winter maneuvers. Next summer it'll be summer maneuvers. Of course there are a few casualties, but everybody knows you can't conduct large scale maneuvers without some injuries. Just don't let anybody tell you there's a war.

MacArthur said there was a simple solution, MacArthur talked to Eisenhower, and that was that. No more war. Even the most bitter diehard Democrat has got to admit these two Republican generals sure did a great job.

As for those tax bills you're getting, forget about 'em. Those are just some old, outmoded tax forms from that terrible New Deal and Fair Deal era. The new administration is going to run the government without taxes. Naturally, if you feel you want to contribute something, just make out a little check to the Collector of Internal Revenue and send it in.

If you feel otherwise, don't bother. Nothing will happen to you. Of course some men might come around and seize your property and throw you in jail, but these are just technicalities. All you've got to do is remember the Republicans are now in, and you know how vigorously they cut taxes.

They cut taxes, that is, in every campaign speech from July till November, and surely by this time there are no taxes left.

It sure is funny to see those stories and pictures in the papers about strikes and violence on the picket lines and such stuff as that. The newspaper people ought to be ashamed of themselves for printing such lies and faked pictures.

Independence Day, 1953, provided the *Irish American* the opportunity to take a respectful look back at the presidency of Harry S. Truman.

Happy Man

July 4, 1953

This Saturday is the Fourth of July, the day we celebrate the anniversary of our Declaration of Independence, when we cut loose from the benevolent protection of Mother England. In 1776 a lot of our forefathers insisted the British were responsible for all our troubles, and in 1953 some of their descendants still feel the same way.

The British do make a convenient punching bag, and they're a long way off, but we ought to face the bare possibility that at least a few of our problems are home made.

One man who thinks they are has been celebrating Independence Day every day since noon on last January 20. He's the man from Independence, Harry S. Truman, and nobody can look at the picture of him taken on a Washington visit last week without knowing Harry's a happy man.

For over five years he did his best at the world's most nearly impossible job. There was a headache every hour on the hour, and a world crisis every Monday, Wednesday and Friday.

As President, Truman was attacked in the daily papers, in magazines, on radio and on television. He was damned if he did and damned if he didn't. They called him an appeaser for not fighting the Communists and a warmonger for actively resisting the Reds' armed aggression.

He was "High Tax Harry" to the Republicans, but this week he could bust his sides laughing at the G.O.P.'s pathetic pleas for Democratic help to avoid a tax cut.

If Truman isn't happy now, there's no happy man alive. He can go where he pleases and do what he wants, and get a friendly reception everywhere. Ex-presidents, of course, get the same treatment from us as ex-heavyweight champions—they are tremendously popular. As champion, Jack Dempsey was booed. As ex-champ, he's one of our best-liked sports figures.

Harry simply has to laugh when he reads of the new Administration's problems. The way the Republicans talked about the situation last fall, everything was going to be so simple—throw the rascals out, get a few hardheaded business men in there to trim the budget and cut taxes, let a military mind solve the military problem of Korea, and so on.

The candidacy of Alabama governor George Wallace for the presidency drew ire in the summer of 1964.

Exit George

August 1, 1964

It's impossible not to feel sorry for a guy who, one day, is riding at the top, and the next has been unceremoniously booted to the bottom.

In the case of George Wallace, however, most of us are willing to make an exception. After all, what's the difference in being at the top of a garbage heap or near the bottom?

Not satisfied with being chosen by the enlightened voters of Alabama to help them maintain their illusion of superiority, Wallace got the dizzy idea of moving to Washington. He began running for President, first as just a symbol of the Hates Rights party, but finally for real.

George was fooled by the votes he got in several states, where he was usually running against a stand-in candidate who did little or no campaigning. Even new as he is in politics, he ought to know anybody who gets his name on the ballot is certain to get some votes—it's only been two years since the supposedly intelligent voters of Jefferson County cast 4,000 ballots for a man who is almost completely illiterate and has long been mentally unbalanced.

While these 4,000 voters could plead ignorance, not knowing the man, those who supported Wallace had no excuse. They were for the Alabaman because they believed as he did—that the all-men-are-created-equal business does not include Negroes. When you speak to such people about the law of the land, they say the law is unconstitutional. When you mention the law of God, they cite Scripture to prove the Almighty intended no such thing.

Anyway, George was riding right at the top, up there with the grapefruit rinds and the chicken bones, until two weeks ago. He was talking about getting on the November ballot in 15 states and winning enough electoral votes to hold the balance of power when the two major candidates fell short.

That was two weeks ago. Where's George now? He's with the guy who left his psychiatrist after a long series of treatments snarling, "Yeah, Doc, you fixed me all right! Before I saw you I was Napoleon—now I'm nobody!"

George has been cast aside like an old heel. Nobody wants him any more, North or South. Why should the Hates

Righters waste their votes on him when they not only have another candidate who thinks as George does, but who has a chance to win all the marbles?

Poor old George. He hasn't got it any more. But then he never did have much, and he was a louse when he had that.

Long-time FBI Director J. Edgar Hoover may have intimidated American presidents but not the *Irish American.*

J. Edgar the Scofflaw
December 3, 1966

About a year ago the editorial columns of some papers, and the letters-to-the-editor department, were filled with scathing denunciations of Dr. Martin Luther King for "encouraging lawlessness and disorder." This was in response to Dr. King's statement that he intended to continue demonstrations, regardless of any laws that said he and his people couldn't.

There were also some pretty bitter blasts against Vice President Humphrey who had said, in effect, that if he were in the position of some minority groups he might want to be part of a rioting mob.

"The law is sacred!"

We will now wait patiently for the same writers of editorials and letters to denounce J. Edgar Hoover.

This week the Justice Department announced that thousands of past and present criminal cases were in jeopardy because the FBI had used wiretaps or other electronic eavesdropping devices.

These wiretaps and other devices are illegal, but that didn't stop J. Edgar Hoover from ordering his agents to use them.

Is not the law just as sacred for J. Edgar as it's supposed to be for Dr. King?

Thirteen years before former actor Ronald Reagan was elected to the presidency, Mike Barry had his eye on him. He did not like what he saw.

Oscar Sure
January 7, 1967

When the Academy Award presentations are made in a couple of months, there may be a special category for actors now in politics. If there is, they can start engraving the Oscar right now for Ronald Reagan. Ronnie boy is a cinch.

Those of you who weren't groggy from what must have seemed, at least to the wives, a dozen straight hours of football Monday, and sat up long enough to watch the news on television, will surely agree that Ronnie was never better.

The Associated Press used a regular reporter instead of a drama critic to cover the inaugural ceremony, so first you must suffer through his dry, factual account:

"Ronald Reagan, one of America's new political stars, became the 33rd governor of California in a colorful post-midnight ceremony and solemnly vowed, 'I'll try very hard.'

"Standing under the Capitol dome, the 55-year-old Republican placed a hand on a 400-year-old Bible and took the oath that gave him the job of solving mounting fiscal and social problems of the nation's most populous state."

If he is successful, it could assure a place in the national political picture for Reagan, the former actor who in his first try for public office defeated Democratic Gov. Edmund G. Brown.

The first thing needed in today's world, for those who watched Reagan's performance, was a little Pepto-Bismol. What a hambone!

To begin with, Reagan did not, as the A.P. man said, recall Benjamin Franklin's words. Not just like that.

Oh no. First he pretended he wasn't sure, that he was depending on his memory ("Was it Franklin or somebody else?") and then he frowned his wonderful boyish frown. Right then you knew Ronnie was a cinch for an Oscar nomination, just on the frown.

The chief executive of the nation's most populous state went bravely on; brave, earnest, sincere. You could see the sincerity oozing out. By George, he WAS able to remember the words of Franklin! Everybody felt real good about that.

After a properly reverent pause, Ronnie continued. Still frowning, of course, and trying oh so hard to find just the right words—"I don't think anyone (slight emphasis on "anyone," brief pause) could ever take office and be so presumptuous (brief pause) to think he could ever do that (longer pause) or that he could follow those precepts completely."

Then he stopped. Ronnie stopped and waited. It takes a good actor to wait, not rush his lines, and Ronnie boy's a good actor.

Finally, looking even more earnest and sincere, he said: "I can tell you this: I'll try very hard. (Pause.) I think it is needed in today's world."

That was it. Ronnie was almost overcome by his own sincerity, but he had managed to get through without breaking down.

All the time, standing at his right hand and making a bold bid for the Best Supporting Actress Award, was Nancy Reagan. Prettier and younger, maybe, than the first Mrs. Ronald Reagan, but not as talented. She'll never even get a nomination—it doesn't take a Helen Hayes to do a three-minute bit as the radiant, adoring wife.

Ronnie himself, though, can start making a place for that Oscar right now. The Academy people just can't overlook a man who, with a month and a half to prepare, still can get up and make his retarded constituents believe he was groping for words to express his thoughts.

It was short, less than a hundred words, duck soup for a man whose whole life had been memorizing words and gestures.

But, as they say in the theatre, there are no small parts—only small actors. Ronnie boy showed what a real actor can do when you give him time to rehearse, how well he used that month and a half to polish this gem.

Yes sir, he worked for his Oscar. It'll be a terrible shame if they don't give it to him just because of what he's getting ready to do to them in his first tax message.

During the 1967 gubernatorial campaign, Republican candidate Louie Nunn's office announced that Ronald Reagan was coming to Louisville to campaign. Mike Barry was on the *qui vive*.

All Bow Low

October 14, 1967

Let's see, now, just how is it a peasant behaves in the presence of royalty? Walk in with eyes lowered, walk backwards when leaving so as not to turn your back on the sovereign ruler, take off your hat . . .

Probably the most important is that business about never asking a question. You are supposed to speak only if royalty talks to you first.

This is the part that can be awkward, particularly if it's supposed to be a press conference, but maybe we members of the lower class can figure out some way to handle this problem.

All of this preparation, of course, is for the visit here Saturday of His Royal Highness Ronald Reagan.

You think it's a joke? Here is the official press release from Republican State Campaign Headquarters, Brown Building, Louisville:

"Judge Louie B. Nunn announced that California's governor, Ronald Reagan, coming to Kentucky on behalf of Nunn, would hold a press conference upon his arrival Saturday, October 14.

"Judge Nunn said, 'Governor Reagan has graciously agreed to hold a press conference upon his arrival here to speak for the Nunn Team. This will be the first conference upon his arrival here to speak for the Nunn Team. This will be the first opportunity for the local Kentucky Press Corps to interview the Governor since his election.' . . ."

Please note the key word in this announcement Reagan has "graciously" agreed to hold a press conference.

All right, you ink-stained wretches, you lousy rabble of low degree, let's shape up! . . .

When you hear all the things he is afraid of, and those he isn't afraid of, and you consider that he conned the kooks in California into electing him governor, and you remember how many kooks there are in the other 49 States, and you know a Republican National convention that would nominate Barry Goldwater and the incredible William Miller is liable to nominate anybody . . .

You've seen the sign posted in some offices: "If You Can Keep Your Head While All About You Are Losing Theirs—It Just Means You Don't Understand the Situation."

That's the way it is with Ronnie-boy. If he doesn't make you afraid, you're out of touch.

5

The Kentucky Political Scene

Kentuckians are notoriously political creatures. Given their constitutional and electoral systems, their primary and general elections, citizens can expect to find their polling places open every six months. The Commonwealth usually elects Democrats both to the governorship and to the state legislature. The only Republican elected to serve as governor of Kentucky (1967-1971) since World War II was Louie B. Nunn.

Not surprisingly, the Democrats in the postwar years factionalized. A.B. "Happy" Chandler (1898-1991) represented the more conservative wing—a faction termed "the Republican wing of the Democratic Party" by Louisville writer Allan Trout. The more liberal or "New Deal" wing of the party was the one toward which the *Irish American* definitely tilted. Its standard bearers were such governors as Earle C. Clements (1896-1985) and Bert Combs (1911-92).

The sage reader will quickly note a particular Barry animus toward Happy Chandler in the excerpts that follow. The *Irish American* used vast quantities of ink—much of it acidic—where Chandler was concerned. Chandler twice served as Kentucky's governor, from 1935 until 1939 and from 1955 until 1959, and he served in the U.S. Senate from 1939 to 1945. He resigned from the Senate to become National Commissioner of Baseball, a position to which team owners declined to reappoint him in 1951. Chandler ran without success for governor in three other campaigns (1963, 1967, and 1971), and sought the Democratic nomination for the presidency in 1956. He remained a controversial force in Kentucky political life until the very end of his life in 1991.

Readers who wish to pursue a more thorough study of Kentucky politics in the postwar years may turn to John Ed Pearce's *Divide and Dissent: Kentucky Politics, 1930-1967* (Lexington: Univ. Press of Kentucky, 1987). For objective accounts of Governors Chandler and Nunn, see the essays by Charles P. Roland (on Chandler) and Robert F. Sexton (on Nunn) in *Kentucky Governors*, ed. Lowell H. Harrison (Lexington: Univ. Press of Kentucky, 1985).

When Louisville and Jefferson County voters turned down a call for a limited constitutional convention to revise Kentucky's 1891 Constitution, the *Irish American* became journalistically livid.

Hang Down Your Heads!

November 12, 1960

We learned something from this campaign. (Hooray! The millions of man-hours and dollars weren't wasted after all!)

Never again will we refer to the literate, intelligent voters of Jefferson County.

Never. Gee, what a bunch of stupes!

Here in the Third District we have SEVENTY THOUSAND people old enough to vote, yet obstinately stupid enough to vote AGAINST the call for a limited constitutional convention.

It ought to be frightening instead of maddening. If we have this many people too lazy to read or too dumb to understand a simple explanation, maybe we ought to forfeit our rights to the democratic process and ask for court-appointed guardians.

Fayette County voted about 17,000 to 9,000 FOR the convention, Jefferson County 70,000 to 60,000 AGAINST the call.

This should be convincing proof that Louisvillians aren't in a class with Lexingtonians for brains, something a lot of us who go to Keeneland have been suspecting for years. (Ever notice the Lexington boys when you walk in, sitting there smacking their lips and saying, "here come the chumps from Louisville to build up the prices for us!"?)

The measure lost by less than 20,000. It is quite obvious where the responsibility lies—right here in Jefferson County.

And not with the Democratic organization or the Republican organization or the candidates. They had their jobs to do and they did them.

The fault lies with the people, those 70,000 miserable muddleheads.

(Need a little Christmas money? Just walk up and down Fourth Street selling the Clark Bridge. You've got 70,000 potential buyers.)

In the wake of the election of Louie Nunn as governor, the *Irish American* predicted a dire course for Kentucky.

Long Drag
November 11, 1967

There's not reason to be surprised. What could you expect from a state that twice elected Chandler?

And, just as they paid dearly for those two mistakes, the citizens of Kentucky will have to pay for their error of Tuesday. They had a rare opportunity to elect an honest, able, qualified, dedicated man for governor. They refused, naturally.

Instead, they chose a man who has always taken the low road, a man of so little principle he has not hesitated to appeal to the worst in men—their fears, their prejudices, their hatreds.

This candidate knew what he was doing. It's been said that if you want to hunt ducks, you go where the ducks are.

Louie Nunn knew where the votes were, and he found them everyplace he looked. Like under rocks.

It is a small comfort to think that Nunn won't have the power the governor usually holds, that he will be unable to leave the state, that he will have to contend with a legislature controlled by the opposition.

Who wants to stand still for four years? This is what Kentucky will be doing, while we go through the mindless charades of ripper bills and accusations and investigations.

The whole miserable mess will add up to the 1971 campaign, which began late Tuesday night.

Kentucky will survive, of course—any state that got through eight years of Chandler is indestructible—but a state as backward as ours desperately needs every minute. And we have just thrown away four years.

The motto of the state is "United We Stand, Divided We Fall."

Look out below!

Mike Barry had been editor of the *Irish American* only a year when Happy Chandler returned to the Kentucky scene after his failure to be reappointed National Commissioner of Baseball. Thus began a pattern of cutting commentary that would last until the paper's last issue, in 1968.

"Martyr" Returns

March 17, 1951

Now we have the martyr back in our midst, bloody but unbowed. Victim of a "sneak attack" by his employers, Albert Benjamin "Happy" Chandler has returned to the promised land, there to wait in quiet dignity until his beloved countrymen vote him back into high office.

This is a lot of slush, of course, but it's the story Happy has managed to sell the press and radio all over the country. Everywhere except in Kentucky, that is. Here the people know him a little better.

They know that "sneak attack" he whispers about was just a normal meeting of the sixteen major league owners, conducted under parliamentary law and following established custom and procedure. These sixteen owners had hired Chandler for seven years, but after five years almost half of them had decided he wasn't good enough for the job.

Instead of accepting their decision in the same spirit in which he had taken the $50,000 (later raised to $65,000) sinecure six years ago, Chandler went scurrying over the land, appearing at every public gathering from formal dinners down to a back alley fish fry. Everywhere he put on the same hammy act.

What had he done, he'd ask plaintively. "They won't tell me," he'd say, lips quivering. Then, bravely blinking through his tears, he'd solemnly announce, "Ah have never done anything to hurt baseball!"

This was always good for wild applause from those who never stopped to think, "Why the hell should he? Ain't the bum getting sixty-five thousand a year to HELP baseball?"

Out of office and supposedly out of politics, he had given his moral support to the traitors within his own party. Chandler made no effort to hide his Dixiecrat sympathies, and this at a time when the Democratic party was apparently doomed to defeat and needed all the help it could get.

Now, having bitten the hand that fed him, Chandler arrogantly decides he'll come back,—provided he gets the biggest prize available at the moment. He got away with it, everywhere except here in Kentucky, which is the only place where it counts. The Chicago Tribune sports page even said in a headline, "Governor Holds Post Open For Him."

The Governor ought to hold something open for Chandler, and that's the gate. The same gate Happy walked out of in 1945, and outside of which he chose to stay in 1948.

There may come a day when the inevitable group of malcontents, dissatisfied with the party leadership just as they have a perfect right to be, will look around for someone to run in opposition. They're sure to seek Chandler, hoping his appeal to the masses will still be potent at the polls.

Let them do what they like, but the regular Democratic Party should never invite this bolter back. They are rid of him now, and it's good riddance.

Chandler's claim to have integrated baseball was a constant irritant to Barry.

Never a Dixiecrat, Says Happy

March 5, 1955

In the Louisville Defender, a Negro weekly, A.B. "Happy" Chandler was quoted in the Feb. 24 issue that he had never given any support to the Dixiecrat movement in 1948.

"I wasn't in politics at the time. I was baseball commissioner," said Chandler. "I never uttered a sound. If anyone can find I uttered a sound, I will resign. The fellow who ran my newspaper, Orville Baylor, ran the Dixiecrat campaign here. When I came back (after the commissioner's job) I kicked him out and Clements gave him a job. And they (the Administration) still got him."

Asked by the Defender about his attitude toward negro problems in the State, Chandler said, "Take a look at my record. I consider all my people just the same. I put Jackie Robinson in baseball and told them to treat him like any other player."

Apparently baseball historians will have to do some rewriting. Until Chandler took the credit, it was generally believed Branch Rickey put Jackie Robinson in baseball.

But Happy says he did it, and you know how Happy would never claim credit for something he didn't do.

Never, no never.

Well, hardly ever.

The Motto of the Oxford Crew

August 13, 1955

When Chandler won the gubernatorial primary on August 6, 1955, the editor of the *Irish American* was, to put it mildly, displeased. His lengthy editorial response to the election of April 13, 1955, was headed "Backward March." It ended with a single phrase many subscribers found mysterious. It read:

"Ours is the motto of the Oxford crew."

Mike Barry's brother Joseph has noted for posterity that a considerable number of inquiries about the phrase poured into the newspaper's office.

He also has provided for the same posterity a free rendering of the Motto as follows: "it is better to lose with the virtuous than win with the bastards."

When Chandler's name was being considered as a favorite son candidate for the presidency as the 1956 Chicago Democratic convention drew near, Barry delivered—in the last line below—his most famous political quip.

Democrats Can Still Lose

June 16, 1956

With the Republicans minus Cooper looking like a lost cause in Kentucky, the Democratic nomination for the Senate seat virtually amounts to just that. It will be a hard race to lose, but still the Democrats can perform the trick the Republicans used to be famous for—snatching defeat from the jaws of victory.

First, piously singing "Harmony, Sweet Harmony," they can climb in bed with Chandler. Letting Happy represent Kentucky at the Democratic National Convention, and telling the nationwide television audience that he is our "favorite son," would drive many real Democrats to the sidelines in November. The independent voters who now eagerly support the party's fight against Chandler would immediately switch to the Republican side.

That's one way to lose. Any time Chandler is referred to in Chicago as "Kentucky's favorite son," it should be made unmistakably clear that the sentence is incomplete.

When the Democrats gathered in Chicago, the *Irish American* maintained, Kentucky had sent them something no other state could offer.

Laugh, Clown, Laugh

August 18, 1956

Come on, fellow Kentuckians. Heads up!

There's no need to be ashamed. In the great drama unfolding this week in Chicago, our state has made its contribution. We've been part of the show.

In nearly all the great plays, even in most of Shakespeare's tragedies, the audience is always given a laugh or two. Sometimes the tension becomes more than the mind can endure, so the dramatist thoughtfully provides the light touch known as comic relief.

Every show, in other words, must have its clown.

Let the other 47 states and the territories provide the leaders, the statesmen, the thinkers.

We have sent A.B. Chandler.

When Chandler returned to Kentucky after the Chicago convention without a nomination, the paper was in no mellower a mood.

Moby Dick Swims Home
August 25, 1956

On August 18 Ol' Blubberboy returned to Frankfort. "Openly crying," reported Allan Trout, "he was too choked with emotion to begin his response at once . . . appeared tired beyond the limits of human endurance. Mrs. Chandler quickly moved to one side of him, and Waterfield to the other. The lieutenant governor grasped him firmly by the arm."

Chandler blubbered to the people at the station that he hadn't been treated fairly at Chicago (can a clown expect anything but laughs?) and repeated his fantastic claim that he could have won—if the convention had deadlocked.

Of course he could have won. A jackass could win the Derby, provided they let a jackass enter and all the thoroughbreds fell down.

Back in his office, Chandler began moaning over a Courier-Journal editorial. The C-J writer had not only stuck the harpoon deep in old Moby Dick, but twisted the barb, and the Big Wail of Kentucky Politics spouted angry, bloody froth.

Obviously this rough game has gotten too rough for Mama's boy. He can't stand the gaff.

Go call Captain Ahab, somebody. This big hunk of blubber's ready to be hauled in.

To Mike Barry's chagrin, the monks of Gethsemani Abbey in Nelson County seemed susceptible to the charms of Happy Chandler.

Chandler Strong at Gethsemane

June 15, 1957

There are some interesting figures in the final returns from the May 28 primary, in which Doris Owens overwhelmingly defeated Chandler's candidate, J.L. "June" Suter, for Clerk of the Court of Appeals.

In Nelson County there are 32 precincts. Miss Owens won 28 of the 32, carrying the county 2,668 to 1,198.

One of the four Suter won was the Trappist Monastery. There the vote was 168 for Chandler's man, only 39 for Miss Owens.

The Monastery also gave Chandler's candidate for state senator, Frank B. Wilson, 196 and his opponent 19.

Sam Houtchens, a Chandler-backed candidate for representative, got 152 votes from the Trappists, his opponent Alvan Wells 53. This result was considered quite unusual by our Bardstown correspondent, who describes Wells as "a devout Catholic" and Houtchens as a man once friendly to the Ku Klux Klan.

This shows the Trappists don't vote along religious lines.

Unfortunately, it also shows how these men, living a cloistered life, are quite susceptible to the solemn promises of a high-ranking outsider. A visitor who appears properly noble and sanctimonious, and who praises the Almighty in almost every sentence, can easily win their innocent hearts.

They are trusting souls, these monks. They are charitable

to all, unwilling to believe there are men who practice deceit. The Bard said, "A man can smile and smile, and be a villain," but with the Trappists a smiling man who thanks God with every breath for a chance to serve "Mah people" is a knight in shining armor. Even if the armor bulges a little and strains at the rivets.

Besides, there was that little matter of a road back to the Monastery. A shame, really that visitors had to travel a route so badly neglected by the highway department.

"Ah will take care of it," the smiling visitor said.

So the monks took care of him. One hundred and sixty-eight votes for Suter, thirty-nine for Miss Owens.

An editorial at election time 1959 gave editor Barry the opportunity to assess at one writing the three "C"s of Kentucky Democratic politics of that era: Chandler, Clements, and Combs. Combs had just been elected governor, with Wilson Wyatt as lieutenant governor.

Congratulations or Sympathy?
November 7, 1959

If you stop to think about it a little bit, you don't know whether to congratulate Combs and Wyatt or send them cards of sympathy. What a mess they're inheriting!

In eight years, under Clements and Wetherby, Kentucky made slow and steady progress. These two men worked hard to make our poor and backward state less poor and less backward.

Then Chandler, as this paper warned in 1955 came in and used the office of governor solely to promote his own selfish interests. . . . Anything he did that helped Kentucky was coincidental, because it was designed only to help Chandler. He wanted national attention, and every act was a calculated move in his illogical, hopeless, ridiculous pursuit of the White House.

Now Combs and Wyatt face the long, arduous job of cleaning up the chaos Chandler left behind. Restoring dignity and decency to the state government will be quick and easy, for they are dignified, decent men, but putting the state's finances in order is an appalling task.

One of the unusual things about this long campaign, both in the primary and the general election, has been the attempt to portray Earle Clements as a villain. Last January, when Wilson Wyatt made the Democratic victory possible by sacrificing his own ambition to be governor, the Louisville man was attacked as having sold his soul to the devil—a devil named Clements.

Bert Combs was attacked as a man being led around by Clements and told what to do and what to say. It is surprising to find so many people who still believe this. These people are in for a shock. Combs, as he will surely demonstrate early and often during his term, is influenced only by one man—Bert Combs. He's a reasonable man, but he's stubborn, mighty stubborn.

The arguments ran, "Combs is run by Clements—and you know the sort of man Earle Clements is!"

Certainly. He's a man who was a judge, a congressman, a governor and a United States Senator. In every one of these offices he was honest and efficient, a glutton for work and afraid of nobody.

In the great game of politics, Earle Clements is a big leaguer. He has struck out on occasion and he's thrown to the wrong base, but his batting average is high and he's fielded some mighty difficult chances. There isn't a team in the country that wouldn't be glad to have him.

Disagreeing with Clements' views is easy. His friends do it all the time, and some of their disagreements are long, loud, and bitter, but they never lose their respect for the man.

Getting a promise or a commitment out of Earle Clements is no more difficult than stopping Jimmy Brown at the line of scrimmage. But, once he gives his word, any bank in Kentucky will cheerfully accept it as collateral.

Earle Clements can be tough, unyielding, difficult and sometimes impossible, but he's no villain. The more men of his type we have in government, the better government we'll have.

Mike Barry could not have planned the scenario any better himself. In the autumn of 1966, Chandler compared himself to Winston Churchill. The *Irish American* was waiting to pounce.

Old Refrain

September 24, 1966

There's a lovely melody played about this time of year, provided you can tune in a radio station that doesn't specialize in bleats and moans to the accompaniment of garbage cans being rolled down a driveway.

This nostalgic old standard is "September Song," the story of a man who wants to marry a girl much younger. He tells her he's in the September of his life, the days have dwindled down to a precious few, and these precious few days he'd like to spend with her. Of course a lot of old men have the same idea, only they don't present it so beautifully.

We've been thinking how appropriate it would be if Albert Benjamin Chandler used this as his campaign song. You know he has decided to run again for governor, having filed his papers Wednesday at Frankfort for the Democratic primary in 1967. Chandler's days have dwindled down to a precious few, but once more into the breach . . . Our state breast stroke champion is 68. "As for being too old," he said Wednesday, "there'd be no British empire today if they had chloroformed Churchill at 65. Adenauer is OK for West Germany at 87, and De Gaulle is not doing too bad in France at 76."

Truer words were never spoken. Certainly not by Chandler.

Even his bitterest enemy (all right, all right, stop the shoving and get in line like everybody else!) must admit Chandler's chances of being elected next year are as good as Adenauer's or De Gaulle's. Of their being elected Governor of Kentucky . . . that is.

Also he seems to have an edge on Churchill.

Incidentally, his typically tasteful reference to chloroforming Churchill leads to the inevitable parallel; what if they had chloroformed Chandler at 35?

There would still be a Kentucky today, and a far more prosperous Kentucky. Our state would not have had to struggle for 25 years without sufficient revenue, simply because that was one perennial candidate's only issue—against the sales tax. The U.S. Senate, major league baseball, bush league football all would have been better off.

As the *Irish American* was itself going down for the count, it published a letter said to have come from Happy Chandler himself.

Refusing to let Chandler have the last word, the paper's response was sarcastically, but effectively, expressed both in the subheading to Chandler's letter that read "Sweet Singer of Versailles Laments Paper's Passing" and in the footnotes to the letter itself.

It shouldn't have been a surprise. After all the years he spent filling this space, we should have known the man wouldn't let the final two issues go by without making at least one more contribution.

Here it is:

A.B CHANDLER
Elm Street
Versailles, Kentucky

November 18, 1968

Mr. Michael Barry
The Kentucky Irish American
325 East Breckenridge[1]
Louisville, Kentucky

My dear Michael:

I am a bit sad to read of the pending demise of the Kentucky Irish American. You know, a great many years ago

I promised Mrs. Chandler that I would be a success in politics and business, and she promised, at the same time, to keep me modest.[2]

I hope I can say, with becoming modesty, that I have made a reasonable success in politics and in business and Mama has done her level best to keep her part of the bargain.[3] Of course, this has been difficult. But, from time to time, she has had an abundance of help from the Kentucky Irish American. Could you possibly give me any advice with respect to advising her whom to turn to now for help?[4]

My family owns and publishes the Woodford Sun at Versailles. We will be 100 years old next year,[5] and we have always felt that it was proper to speak softly with respect to nearly everyone, especially those who were about to depart from us.

I knew your father quite well. I thought he was a splendid gentleman. I have always regretted that, somehow, it was not possible for you to accord me that same treatment that he gave me during his lifetime, which was generous.[6]

I imagine the Courier-Journal might have a good word for you, too, now, although I cannot recall that in times past they have considered it their life mission to say anything complimentary concerning you, the Irish American, or your humble[7] servant.

Nonetheless, I am sincere[8] when I say that I hate to see the Irish American depart from the Kentucky scene. Even with its opposition, I have prospered beyond my due.[9] I still feel that God is in His Heaven, even though all is not right in the world. You have my best wishes[10] for your success in your new endeavors.

Yours very truly,

Albert B. Chandler

P.S. I hope sincerely that the information that I was about to locate an office in Louisville had nothing to do with the decision to close the Irish American.[11] Perhaps you thought having the two of us active there was more than the other critics could stand.

A.B.C.

* * *

1. You misspelled Breckinridge.

2. Mrs. Chandler has kept you as modest as you were the day you were born. That day you had no modesty at all, and in 70 years you have never acquired a smidgin.

3. You were a bargain?

4. Ann Landers.

5. Try for another 100; maybe in that time you could produce one readable issue.

6. Father was indeed a generous man, a charitable man. On occasion, his generosity and charity overwhelmed his judgment.

7. Humble? You make Charles de Gaulle seem like Charlie Brown.

8. You couldn't be more sincere. Of course you couldn't be any less, either.

9. Way beyond.

10. You have always been generous with good wishes. Also with unsolicited advice and hindsight observations. None of these are spendable.

11. It did not. A big factor in our decision to close was your announcement (No. 236 in the series) that you would never again run for public office. What good is a slingshot when the blimp stops flying?

6

The Kennedy Years

The presumption would seem to be a ready one: an Irish Catholic Democratic editor, looking toward the 1960 presidential campaign, would enthusiastically support John F. Kennedy. Not so of Mike Barry at the *Kentucky Irish American*, at least not in the beginning. His choice, rather, was Adlai Stevenson. As for Kennedy? A fine fellow, he said, but too young and too Catholic for a realistic run.

Barry, always kindly disposed toward JFK the man, warmed to him in the presidency. He supported the president's stance in demanding a price rollback from U.S. Steel in 1962, his handling of the Cuban Missile Crisis, and his proposal for a nuclear nonproliferation treaty in 1963. When the young president was assassinated on November 22, 1963, the *Irish American* eulogized him in one of its most memorable and moving tributes.

In the summer of 1958, Mike Barry sought to rebut a column by nationally syndicated columnist Joseph Alsop arguing for a Kennedy candidacy.

Dreamer Joe

August 30, 1958

Columnist Joseph Alsop wrote this week: "The New York story raises the question . . . whether Senator Kennedy's national candidacy will be helped or hurt by his religion, which played such a large role in the political fortunes of the great Al Smith. This is a problem that every student of the Democratic form-sheet for 1960 argues about in private. This seems like a good time to discuss it straightforwardly in public.

"After prolonged inquiry among the professionals of many states, this reporter has reached the somewhat unorthodox conclusion that the same religious affiliation which so handicapped Al Smith will be a positive advantage to Jack Kennedy.

"In the first place, thank God, the country is still ashamed of the campaign of prejudice that was waged against Smith. If anything of that sort is again attempted, it will win a Catholic candidate more sympathy-votes than it can cost in prejudice votes.

"Secondly, the Protestant American view of the Catholic Church has greatly changed in the last three decades . . . This so-called 'better element' will not fight another Catholic candidate as they fought Smith, just because he was a Catholic . . .

"Thirdly . . . the organized prohibitionists have all but vanished from the American political scene. . . .

"One cannot imagine great numbers of our farming people, even in the Protestant South, rallying once again to the 'hate-the-Pope' battle cry . . ."

After prolonged inquiry among the professionals of this state, it is our considered opinion that Alsop is living in a dream world.

For one thing, most students of political history believe Al Smith's religion was not the decisive factor in 1928. Just as no Republican could have won four years later, no Democrat could have won then. The people believed they were voting for a continuance of what was called Coolidge prosperity, and they weren't yet sick enough of the Prohibition farce to support a wet.

Smith's religion hurt him, undoubtedly, but it just made certain defeat a slaughter. Kennedy's religion would make a certain Democratic victory in 1960 highly uncertain.

Ignorance has not yet been banished from the land, and where there is ignorance there is prejudice. Alsop's contention that "the country is still ashamed" of what went on in 1928 is nonsense.

What's more, the young Senator would be opposed by many high-minded Americans, completely free from religious prejudice, yet sincerely believing that no Catholic President could be objective on various public questions, such as Federal aid to education.

It would be nice to believe this country has reached the advanced stage of enlightenment where a man's race or creed or color would not affect his candidacy for public office.

Nice, but foolish. The time is not yet.

Senator Kennedy himself got wind of the "Dreamer Joe" editorial and wrote the *Irish American* asking for a complete copy. Here editor Barry printed the Kennedy note and reviewed his own reservations and concerns.

Kennedy Monopolizes Political News
March 28, 1959

Most of the national political news is being made these days by the young Senator from Massachusetts. On the righthand side of this page is a summary of what editors of Catholic papers thought of Kennedy's statements in Look Magazine earlier this month.

The Senator is also mentioned favorably, quite favorably, in the Manchester Guardian Weekly. We will get to that in a minute, but first you may be interested in the following:

"Washington, D.C.
March 9, 1959

"Editor
Kentucky Irish American:

"Recently I read an editorial commenting on your January editorial regarding Joseph Alsop's speculation about the election of a Catholic to the Presidency. I would greatly appreciate your sending me a copy of your editorial and would be glad to have any comments you care to make.

"With every good wish, I am,

Sincerely
John F. Kennedy."

* * *

The editorial Senator Kennedy mentioned was not January, but in our Aug. 30, 1958, issue. Joseph Alsop had written: "After prolonged inquiry among the professionals of many states, this reporter has reached the somewhat unorthodox conclusion that the same religious affiliation which so handicapped Al Smith will be a positive advantage to Jack Kennedy . . . The country is still ashamed of the campaign of prejudice that was waged against Smith. If anything of that sort is attempted, it will win a Catholic candidate more sympathy-votes than it can cost in prejudice-votes."

The Kentucky Irish American said Alsop was living in a dream world, pointing out that most political historians believe Smith's religion was not a major factor in 1928. What's more, Alsop's belief that the country is still ashamed is impossibly naive.

In the first place, half the people who voted 31 years ago are no longer alive. Of those still kicking who did vote for Hoover, many were Republicans who had voted for Harding and Coolidge, and stayed with the G.O.P. out of habit. Others voted against Smith because he opposed Prohibition. Some disliked the way he talked, or were against New Yorkers in general.

By the time you get down to the people who voted against Al Smith because he was a Catholic, have since repented, and are now willing to forget all their other convictions and vote for Kennedy in the way of atonement, you haven't got enough votes to carry a precinct.

* * *

Anyway, a copy of the Aug. 30 issue was sent to Senator Kennedy, together with a note saying that the six months elapsing since then had produced no change in the editor's mind. (This is rather remarkable, in that the same mind has been known to change four times from the minute they step on the track until they're in the gate.)

Back came a letter of thanks, dated March 18, from Stephen E. Smith, apparently one of the Senator's administrative assistants. That's nice work if you can get it, and he's got it. Smith added:

> "We regret that your opinion is unchanged. It has been our experience that Alsop's point is well taken. A recent independent poll of eight western states showed the Senator receiving a greater percentage of the Protestant vote than either Humphrey or Symington. It has also been our observation that the sentiment you voice is most often heard from Catholic and Jewish sources. It would seem that this is the result of their difficulties in the past years as minority groups."

Well, now, isn't that sweet of Smitty to be so considerate? We poor Catholics—and some of our Jewish friends—can't see the big, broad picture because we've suffered as minority groups. Real nice of Smitty to straighten out our warped thinking.

We don't know who else Kennedy's got in his office, but if they're all like this stuffy, patronizing bum the Senator really needs help.

You've been too long indoors, Smith. Why don't you get out in the fresh air—and take with you a kite and a big ball of string?

During election week 1960, the *Irish American* urged Catholics to remember not only that they had been the victims of intolerance, but that many Protestants had been courageous in their defense. In the election, Kennedy won Louisville city precincts but lost in Jefferson County by fewer than 1,000 votes. Nixon won the vote in Kentucky.

Something for Catholics to Remember

November 5, 1960

The uproar over religion in this campaign has affected Catholics in different ways. Some have been annoyed, some amused, some furious.

Almost all Catholics, however, have been astounded. They knew there was a certain element of prejudice, but they never dreamed it was so widespread and so bitter. The things some people believe!

But it has been a wonderfully heartwarming experience to see so many Protestants spring to their defense. When the time came to stand up and be counted, Protestants all over the country have had the courage of their convictions. They have steadfastly refused to take the easier road of silence.

This is something Catholics should remember, something Catholics must remember. What these Protestants have done has been right, but it has not been easy. As Andrew Jackson said, one man with courage makes a majority, but standing alone can be a painfully trying experience. Many Protestants defending a Catholic's constitutional rights have been denounced by their neighbors, their friends, their business associates, their fellow church members.

If you're a Catholic, remember this. And ask yourself if you would have had the same moral courage.

Picking the winner next Tuesday ought to be easy. As we have been reminded the past few weeks, Jefferson County hasn't been wrong on a Presidential election in fifty years.

Therefore pick the candidate that carries the Third District of Kentucky and you have picked the next President of the United States. (Or the county has goofed for the first time in half a century.)

A month ago this column said that while the issue might be in doubt across the country, there was no question but that the Democrats would carry Jefferson County.

The truth is we weren't aware of the county's record in picking Presidents when we made that prediction, but now that we know it still goes. It is our calculated guess that Kennedy will carry Jefferson County by a minimum of 10,000, probably more.

Naturally this means we think Kennedy will be elected. We do.

It is the belief here that Kennedy has that certain quality, rare among candidates, to attract votes. Votes by the bushel, the bale, the carload.

Roosevelt had it. So did Alben Barkley. Here at home Charley Farnsley has that certain something.

It doesn't necessarily mean the candidate has outstanding ability or qualifications, although FDR did and Farnsley has. Eisenhower, for instance, is the nearest thing to no President the country has had since Coolidge, and yet if Ike were eligible he could keep on getting elected by landslides until he died. (After which the Republicans would have him stuffed and win a couple of more before the people discovered there was a difference. There would be, of course. Absolutely. Oh, stop asking questions!)

When Kennedy faced down "big business" in the spring of 1962, the paper was ready with its support.

Big Steal
April 14, 1962

Woodrow Wilson spoke out against that "little group of wilful men." Now John Fitzgerald Kennedy, his Irish up for the first time in public, has denounced a "tiny handful of steel executives."

At this writing the President and the Attorney General and members of Congress are all figuring what they can do about steel prices to protect the country's interests. It may develop that they can do nothing, the constitutional rights of private enterprise being what they are, but the one thing certain is that Kennedy has the country behind him. Reaction across the land is tremendous and still snowballing, the people solidly supporting the young Chief Executive. Public opinion may yet bring a victory.

Veteran political writers said only one other President has displayed such anger in public—Roosevelt the day after Pearl Harbor. In a sense, this is the same thing, because Kennedy's brief, bitter statement was also a declaration of war. He believes the country has been attacked. The President intends to fight back.

There is a sharp contrast between Kennedy's attitude toward "big business" and that of his predecessor. Ike stood in awe of the giants of industry. They were his golfing companions, his bridge partners. He sought their advice and valued their counsel—obviously anybody smart enough to run General Motors was smart enough to run the country.

Men with money don't impress Kennedy at all. For one thing, very few of them had as much as his father, and in the fine job he did raising his family the elder Kennedy taught his sons and daughters to rate character and brains and talent above a bank account.

It should also be noted that in this instance, for one of the few times since the New Deal changed the pattern, big business has become the villain. Almost always before it has been the unions—John L. Lewis during the war, aircraft industry strikes, railroad brotherhoods, Cape Canaveral work stoppages.

Now we have the old big business image of the Teddy Roosevelt era—greedy, grasping, selfish men, ruthlessly crushing the workers.

The steel executives are everything Kennedy said. They're also something else—stupid. Don't these men know where they are, and what time it is?

After John Kennedy was shot to death in Dallas, wrote the *Irish American* in its eulogy-editorial, there were none to offer sympathy, for the entire nation was in mourning.

Mourners All

November 30, 1963

It was a death in the family, but there was no one to offer sympathy, no one to bring comfort.

When the hardest blow of all comes, your neighbors and

friends and relatives are quick to respond. They come to help you bear the heavy burden, to do the little they can. They all say, "If there's anything I can do . . ." and you know if there were they would do it.

This time there were no neighbors or friends or relatives, because the death was in all their families, too.

There was a wake in every house along the block, on all the streets of all the towns over all this grieving land.

If there were homes where there was no grief, those who live in them are to be pitied, for if a man cannot know sorrow, neither can he know joy.

This President was a member of every family. He was never a distant, far-off figure, to be read about in connection with the business of government or glimpsed occasionally at some solemn ceremonial affair.

He was with us so many times, in so many ways.

In some families he was a son, in others a father. Or a brother. Or the next-door neighbor so close he was really part of the family.

And we were all part of his family. We shared his pride in his wife, his joy in his children. The respect and affection he gave his parents, the fierce loyalty for his brothers, were for all of us a shining example.

He never asked us for anything—except our best. He wanted this land of the free and home of the brave to be just that, a land where every man was free, and every man brave enough to stand up for justice.

He never asked us for anything he wasn't willing to give himself—and always he gave his best.

He gave us courage, and inspiration, and hope.

And, finally, he gave us all there was to give, all that any man could give.

He gave himself.

The Good Lord will take care of this good man, John Kennedy, just as He takes care of all good men.

Let us pray that He continues to watch over the rest of us, for indeed these are perilous time.

There is the enemy without, and the enemy within. Either can destroy us.

There was hope that the danger from the enemy without had been lessened. Just over a year ago Khrushchev had tested Kennedy, dared him, challenged him—and he had the challenge hurled back in his teeth. Khrushchev had to retreat, and his withdrawal would have been even more humiliating had not Kennedy wisely allowed him to save a measure of face.

Since that dark hour, when the slightest hesitation—or the slightest rashness—could have plunged us into World War III,the tension has been slowly easing. Slowly, yes, but definitely.

Now it can build up all over. Khrushchev does not know President Johnson. He does know our allies cannot possibly place the same trust and confidence in Kennedy's successor. Khrushchev may test one of them—or he may test us again.

The cornerstone of world peace—Khrushchev's knowledge that Kennedy could not be pushed—has been removed. Thus the whole structure is endangered, and shoring it up will take time. The question is how much time there is.

Then there is the danger from within, a clear and present danger. We have among us people who may not be willing to die for what they believe, but they're ready to kill.

These are the people who believe that the Lord, who made us all, made them superior. To maintain this mythical superiority, they will do anything.

They will use bullets, usually in the back, or bombs, planted in the dead of night. They will use food as a weapon, depriving a man of his job, his chance to earn a living. They will take away the only way he knows to put bread into the mouths of his children.

Or they will use their ballots, electing candidates who cunningly capitalize on their hate by promising to keep them superior.

Then we have the cowards who lack the courage to live with danger from without. They have one solution for all problems—war. A war that someone else will fight in, someone else will die in. These are people who do not realize that after World War III there cannot possibly be World War IV, because there won't be enough world left to fight over. It will be a place, someone has said "where the survivors will envy the dead."

Because they are sore afraid, because their small minds cannot accept unending tension as a way of life, they cry for action. They charge the peacemakers with cowardice or treason—or both. We have the strength now, they say, to destroy those who will attack us later. Waiting is folly, talk is treason—let us demand instant, unconditional surrender or we shall unleash our terrible swift sword.

This is madness. We cannot fight, we cannot surrender. Neither can we demand surrender. All we can do is what men of good will have always done—work unceasingly to lessen the danger. If a thousand hours of patient negotiating across a table produce nothing, be ready to talk another thousand, and another.

So long as we talk, we will not shoot. Nor will our enemies. It is when the talking stops, when men will no longer try to understand each other, that the end is at hand.

And who can say that somewhere, somehow, these men will not find the way to lasting peace?

When Robert F. Kennedy was killed in Los Angeles in June 1968, the *Irish American* told its readers in a subheadline: "Tragedy in California Is Dallas Nightmare All Over."

Darkest Day
June 8, 1968

We have no words of our own to write, or to say. Except, perhaps, a few prayers, but even these must be said with faint hopes. How can we dare ask the Lord to take care of a people so filled with hate?

The Wall Street Journal asks, "Is this murderous attempt yet another sign that American society as a whole is profoundly and uniquely sick with violence?"

A professor of psychiatry at Harvard answers, "Since violence seems to be a feature of our national scene, it probably increases the likelihood that an individual with personal mental problems will use violent expression rather than vocal expression."

Bernard Kempler, professor of psychology at Emory University, Atlanta: "To a lot of people, violence has become acceptable, and assassination a logical political act. Even if the people who shot President Kennedy and Dr. King were emotionally motivated individual assassins, they swim in a public mood that makes these shootings meaningful to them."

Dr. Stephen Groshart of Los Angeles probably expressed the thoughts of many when he said, "I get the feeling that we're on a runaway train or something—that the country has gone over the edge and there's nothing I or anyone can do about it. It's a paralyzing sort of despair. What in God's name has happened to us?"

A lot of things, some that have happened and some that we have caused to happen, but few of them in God's name.

7

The Civil Rights Movement

The old historical adage is largely true: Kentucky and Louisville "went southern" after the Civil War. From Appomattox until the 1890s, most of Kentucky's governors—as well as Louisville's governing elite—were men who had Confederate credentials or sympathies. A large Confederate monument built in that era will be found in Louisville today, but it is matched by no Union monument.

Louisville's segregation patterns continued well into the twentieth century, as detailed by historian George Wright in *Life Behind a Veil*. Under the terms of Kentucky's 1904 Day Law, even the University of Louisville was off-limits to African-American students until 1950. The 1960s brought dramatic demonstrations and disputes in the city, resulting in landmark civil rights legislation.

The Louisville Board of Aldermen passed a public accommodations ordinance in May 1963 barring discrimination in restaurants and businesses. The most controversial struggle of all locally came over the open housing ordinance, eventually passed by the Board of Aldermen, in December 1967. This last act was successful because of the support of many community and church groups, both black and white, a newly elected Board of Aldermen, and the *Courier-Journal* and other media, including the *Kentucky Irish American*.

As early as 1950, the *Irish American* was urging local Democrats to seek the election of an African-American to the Board of Aldermen.

Democrats Should Name Negro

December 30, 1950

With a long, long list of offices to be contested in the coming election, you can look for a long, long list of candidates. They are sure to start popping soon. Nobody wants to be the first out, and nobody wants to be left out, either. As soon as one brave man takes the plunge you'll see a mad scramble.

It is therefore the proper time for the Democratic Party here to take a positive stand on the question of a Negro candidate for the Board of Aldermen. As citizens and taxpayers, the Negroes of Louisville are certainly entitled to representation on the Board, and from a political standpoint, they long ago earned the right to a place on the Democratic ticket.

A long delay while the leaders duck and dodge this question will mean only one thing, that the Democrats don't want a Negro alderman. This time the Negro Democrats, who have worked so long and loyally in the past, are not going to be satisfied with excuses.

The duty of the Democratic Party here is clear. It remains to be seen whether or not the leaders will measure up to their responsibilities.

When the popular local amusement facility Fontaine Ferry resisted integration of its park and swimming pool in 1961, the *Irish American* stood aside from its general liberalism in racial matters. "Schools, restaurants . . . yes. Swimming pools, no." It added, "Naturally, this is only a question of time."

Hot Water

June 24, 1961

The Fontaine Ferry Park trouble has been the big integration story the past week. We have had pictures, news reports, editorials, ultimatums, closed-door discussions and everything else, but nobody yet has mentioned the one big stumbling block.

It's the swimming pool.

Fontaine Ferry, as all residents of this area know, is the community's one and only amusement park complete with roller coaster, merry-go-round and other youthful delights.

It is in the West End, the section of Louisville where more and more Negro families are buying homes. These families, particularly their younger members, want to go in Fontaine

Ferry and ride the roller coaster and the captive airplanes and the rest. What kid, standing on the outside and looking in, wouldn't?

They probably don't care much about swimming in the Fontaine Ferry pool, but obviously the management of this privately-owned park cannot admit Negroes to the rest of the place and bar them from the pool. (Another thing to consider is Gypsy Village, the open air dance floor adjoining the park on the south side.)

It has already been demonstrated, in the pools in our city parks, that the great majority of white citizens are not yet ready to accept integrated swimming. Schools, restaurants, golf courses, tennis courts, playgrounds—yes. Swimming pools, no.

Naturally this is only a question of time. Changes in our social patterns that would not even have been mentioned a few years ago are now accepted without question. Further changes are inevitable.

But the issue is what to do now. The Fontaine Ferry management has indicated, by its refusal to admit Negroes, that it prefers to wait. The management believes opening up now would mean a complete change from all-white patronage to all-Negro. This could mean more profits, less profits, or no profits. Inasmuch as it is Fontaine Ferry's investment at stake, it would seem only fair that Fontaine Ferry be allowed to reach its own decision.

The Negro integration steering committee, led by Bishop C. Ewbank Tucker and Frank Stanley, Jr., say that Fontaine Ferry should be opened up now.

The Courier-Journal and Times think the same thing. In an editorial deploring violence last weekend at the park, the Times said: "The goal the pickets sought was admission to the park on the same basis as anybody else. In our opinion it is a just and proper one . . ."

Juvenile Court Judge Henry A. Triplett, who has been trying to lay down ground rules for integration demonstrations, also agreed with the Negro leaders and the two local papers. "I am aware," he said, "that much of the blame here is the refusal of Fontaine Ferry to admit people of the Negro race and I don't condone that for a minute."

So far the Courier-Journal and Times have found nothing unjust or improper about the refusal of other privately-owned lakes and pools and swim clubs to integrate, perhaps because none of these have had to make a decision.

This complete integration, too, is just a question of time. All restrictions will be removed at the Country Club, the Pendennis, Lakeside, Richmond, River Road, Tucker's, Y.M.C.A., Lighthouse . . .

Yes, indeed. Then we can all relax, because there will be no more problems.

A supporter of Dr. Martin Luther King, Jr., Barry was increasingly troubled by certain remarks of the civil rights leader. On this occasion, the editor deflected its critique of King to FBI Director J. Edgar Hoover.

Why the Delay in Denouncing Director?

July 23, 1966

Sometime ago Dr. Martin Luther King, who among his many eloquent speeches has interspersed a few unfortunate remarks, said something about it was all right to break the law.

What Dr. King had in mind, naturally, was the Negroes, in their struggle to obtain the rights and privileges they were supposed to have been born with, sometimes had to break the rules laid down by white supremacists in order to keep Negro citizens in subjugation.

There is no question, of course, but that Dr. King has said and done some foolish things, as who hasn't. His preposterous proposal to go to Viet Nam, for instance. With all his talents, Dr. King is completely without qualification for conducting this country's foreign policy, and he would be well advised to stay in his own country and mind his own store. These days and times it needs minding more than ever.

But Dr. King did not deserve to have his statement about breaking the law so badly distorted and warped and misquoted as it has been, and is still being. There isn't a conservative columnist or radical right rabble rouser in the land who hasn't taken his swing at Dr. King.

He was blamed for the Watts riot. He is currently being blamed for the outbreaks in Chicago and Cleveland and everywhere else. Why, didn't he tell his people it was all right to break the law? What can you expect?

Okay, okay, Dr. King said it. But most of his bitterest critics know very well what he really meant.

What we have been waiting for is that first word or first hint or first indication of any sort from one of the conservative columnists or rabble rousers that J. Edgar Hoover, the Great White Father of the FBI, probably the only man ever to have canonization ahead of embalming (No, he has not been embalmed. It's just the way he looks in those pictures. And the way he sounds when he talks.) . . . did the same thing Dr. King did. He said it was all right to break the law.

The Great White Father's motives were just as noble as Dr. King's too. The law was to be broken in a good cause, so that made it all right.

If you've been reading the papers, you know some of our highest legal authorities are having fits over the admission that FBI agents, acting under guess-who's orders, have been illegally using wiretaps. Inasmuch as they were after criminals—in the world of the FBI any man involved in gambling is a criminal—they were told it was all right to "bug" half the joints in Vegas.

They apparently did a lot of other wiretapping, too, at other times in other places. Prosecuting attorneys fear, and rightly so, that their cases are going to be thrown right out of court when this evidence is introduced. At the moment, it isn't possible to estimate how widespread the damage may be to the normal process of law enforcement.

But J. Edgar said it was all right, just like Dr. King said it was all right.

You can wait, along with us, for one of Dr. King's critics to point out the parallel.

But don't hold your breath.

When Martin Luther King Jr. remarked that America is "the greatest purveyor of violence in the world today," editor Barry decided that the civil rights leader had abdicated his role as national moral leader.

King Abdicates

April 8, 1967

Until this week, it was easy to name the one man in the whole country who had done the most to hurt civil rights.

Stokely Carmichael, of course. Every time this hatemonger stood up and yelled "Black Power!" he recruited members and money for the KKK, the White Citizens's Councils and the Concerned Citizens Committees.

Always those working in the cause of justice would moan, "Why doesn't he talk sense? Why can't he be more like Martin Luther King?"

Well, now he is, but Carmichael hasn't changed. Dr. King has decided to join with Stokely. The two have announced they will participate in a nationwide Vietnam protest on April 15, which is being organized by Dr. King's chief deputy in the Southern Christian Leadership Conference.

In one speech Tuesday, Dr. King managed to make people forget all the wonderful work he has done in the past, lost the respect of those who considered him a man of sound, mature judgment, and pushed Stokely Carmichael out of the running for the MVP Award on the other team.

As the first and foremost advocate of non-violence, as an eloquent spokesman for his people, as a man of demonstrated courage, Martin Luther King has become a national figure, respected even by his enemies.

Now he's thrown it all away. The damage he has done to civil rights can't even be estimated, nor can you assess the hurt Dr. King has done to himself.

He is unhappy about the war in Vietnam. So is every other American, black, white or any shade in between.

He wants us to get out of Vietnam. So does every other American.

But Dr. King doesn't tell us how to get out. Surely he doesn't mean all of our forces should immediately climb on the next boat or the next plane and leave that miserable country, because even Dr. King knows what that would mean. All the people in South Vietnam who have been fighting on our side would be murdered, and there would be no place on the globe where we could find an ally. There might be Americans callous enough for the first, but are they also willing to risk a retreat into isolation?

Up to this point there is no difference between Martin Luther King, John Doe or Richard Roe. The doctor doesn't like the situation but he doesn't know what to do about it.

So he criticizes the U.S. for being involved, and the efforts our government officials have made to get us uninvolved. Even here there is no real difference between Dr. King and Senator Fulbright and Walter Lippmann.

Nobody is going to argue with Dr. King over that, because nobody else is satisfied with what we are doing. Nobody can be, because we haven't succeeded in stopping the shooting. Until we do, our efforts are all failures.

But when Martin Luther King cries out that his country alone is to blame, and his country is "the greatest purveyor of violence in the world today," and that our soldiers are killing mostly children, he is not telling the truth. He is simply parroting the party line from Hanoi. He is spouting nonsense, dangerous nonsense, this overnight expert in foreign policy.

Dr. King has made a fool of himself. And, when he identifies the civil rights movement with the anti-war group in this country, he is giving every white supremacist in the land a fearsome weapon with which to attack his people. Now the rednecks and their sympathizers can wrap themselves in the flag.

It was a great day for the Negroes when they found a leader.

Now it must be a sad day, for they have lost one.

An editorial in March 1967 revealed strong support for passage of an open housing ordinance in the city.

All Three Groups Are Wrong

March 25, 1967

The three local groups most excited over the open housing ordinance are as follows:

1. White homeowners who are afraid Negroes will move onto their block, thus sharply reducing the value of their property.

2. Real estate men who are afraid the clause allowing an individual to handle the sale of his own house will ruin their business.

3. Public officials who are afraid the voters will turn on them no matter what they do.

All three groups are as wrong as they can be. None of the things they're afraid of will ever happen.

1. There are abundant figures to show property values are not reduced solely because Negroes moved into the neighborhood, both here in Louisville and elsewhere around the country.

2. How many individuals are qualified to handle the sale of their own homes? How many would dare try it? No matter how loyal a man feels he must be to the neighbors he's leaving behind, he isn't going to risk losing thousands of dollars just to keep them feeling secure.

3. For every extremist vote he loses, the public official will pick up an extremist on the other side. And the great bulk of citizens who don't let such things change their votes will still decide any election.

Some people around here just never learn. A few years ago they were running around like Chicken Little, screaming of all the terrible things that would happen if Negroes were allowed to go in so-called white restaurants, movies, bars.

Especially bars. In 1963, after the passage of the ordinance barring discrimination in public places, the president of the Louisville Tavern Owners Association wrote to the smaller papers:

"The big newspapers have brought us to the brink of disaster. We are appealing to you and other non-syndicated news publications to lead us back into the peaceful meadows of legal and right . . .

"Our Creator intended for humans, birds and animals to segregate . . .

Then, after comparing the "rowdy and disorderly demonstrations of Negroes," which he called the responsibility of the big syndicated papers, to "the Hitler-Nazi slaughter of millions of innocent people," the tavern group president quoted figures:

"The 10 per cent Negro population could systematically torch-burn every white home in America within one hour . . .

"The 88 per cent white population could murder every Negro in America within the hour . . .

"The time has come to draw the racial issue—not tomorrow, but today . . ."

Under such inspired leadership, the tavern owners went to court to fight the ordinance. Some of them were so emotional they had even the level-headed operators believing terrible things would happen if it became legal for Negro citizens to drink in the same bars with whites

They lost their case in court, the bars were opened, and you know what happened.

Nothing.

When the housing ordinance is finally passed, with enough legal teeth to make it effective, the story will be the same.

Nothing will happen. There will be no mass "invasion" of present all-white neighborhoods, no mass exodus of white homeowners because a Negro family moved onto the block.

If nothing is going to change, and nothing is going to happen, why all the sound and fury?

Because this community is no different from any other. Along with the great bulk of normal, peace-loving citizens, we have the inevitable percentage of nuts.

There are the Negro leaders who won't lead, but who invite "technicians" from out of town. These men come here and, instead of helping with the solution, immediately become part of the problem. They say things and do things that destroy the sympathy of citizens who were for their cause, create resentment among neutrals, and inflame the passions of their extremist opponents.

There are those who line up with Concerned Citizens Committee, which can be identified by its initials as readily as the KKK. And as correctly.

If it were possible to send all the out-of-town technicians back out of town, and move the CCC down to Alabama or Mississippi, the rest of us could get on with the unfinished task that lies before us.

This is the job we will never finish, but it's the job on which we must never cease working.

It is to see that "Liberty and justice for all" means what it says.

When the Board of Aldermen failed to pass the open housing ordinance on a first try, the *Irish American* editor was clearly angry.

So Easy, So Simple
April 15, 1967

All the aldermen had to do was pass the ordinance. In its amended form, it probably wasn't strong enough to solve the problems that now exist, but it would have been a step forward. Most important, however, its operation would have demonstrated to the Koncerned Kluxers that their precious southern way of life wasn't going to be affected.

Then they could have taken the bedsheets off their pointed heads, put away their Confederate flags, and gone back to eating eggs with their grits instead of throwing them at marchers.

The community could also have gotten rid of visiting "technicians" and the likes of Dick Gregory, who instead of helping with the solution simply add to the problem.

We could have had a little peace around here. The housing ordinance wasn't going to change anything, any more than the anti-discrimination ordinance affecting restaurants, bars, movies and other public places changed anything. There would only have been a scattered few areas now all white into which Negro families would have moved, in most cases improving the neighborhood. (If you haven't got a white neighbor you'd like to trade, you're lucky.)

Louisville could have continued the progress we have been making for years in peaceful integration.

Everything would have been wonderful, except the aldermen blew it.

It isn't correct to say we're right back where we started. We have lost ground. Now it's just going to take that much longer to do what must be done, and what will be done.

And it will be, in spite of the KK's and the Real Estate Board and the technicians and the Dick Gregory's.

In forecasting a stormy civic summer in 1967, the *Irish American* had praise—faint though it may have been—for the Louisville police for their handling of racial tensions.

Ahead Lies the Summer of Discontent
April 22, 1967

Not so long ago, when we were reading about the terrible things that were happening in Selma and Montgomery and Birmingham, many of us said, "There, but for the grace of God, goes Louisville . . ."

The Lord no longer makes His face to shine upon us. We have not yet reached the depths of Alabama or Mississippi, but we're on our way. From sticks and stones to guns and bullets is but a question of time, and time is running out.

In the whole sorry performance of the present city administration, there is so far only one redeeming bit. That is the way our police have handled these difficult, dangerous situations, from Chief Bindner down to the patrolman of lowest rank. It must be a sore temptation to these officers, charged unfairly with "police brutality" by those they are trying to protect, and the targets of physical and verbal abuse by the white trash that make up these miserable mobs not to take their riot sticks and lay about them.

Actually this has been the only difference between Louisville and those Deep South bastions of bigotry. Here the cops are neutral: down south they're part of the mob.

If spring comes, can a long, hot summer be far behind?

During the turmoil surrounding the open housing debate, rumors circulated about an attempt to disrupt the 1967 Derby. The *Irish American* took a dim view. Its term "nine hunks of solid concrete" referred to the aldermen who voted against the ordinance on April 11, 1967, as it went down to defeat 9-3. The Derby was run practically without incident.

Bridle Party
April 29, 1967

It is not absolutely certain the Kentucky Derby will be run May 6. There could be a fire or a flood or a tornado, or some other such disaster listed as an "act of God" in the insurance policies.

But that's the only way. The Derby positively won't be stopped by an act of man, particularly a man named Gregory or King or Carmichael.

Because he came up with a quotable line, Negro comedian Dick Gregory's threat to stop the Derby has gotten wide publicity. "I ain't going to lay down in front of a horse myself," Gregory said, "but there's a lot of cats that will."

Some of you may remember the story of the mother whose little boy didn't care for spinach. "Why," she urged, "there are lots of little boys who would just love to eat that spinach!"

The little boy looked up at her and said, "Name three."

We doubt Dick Gregory can name three "cats" who will lay down in front of a horse. It is a practice not likely to become habit-forming. Back in 1913, during the running of the Epsom Derby in England, a woman ran out on the track and grabbed the bridle of the king's horse, causing a spill.

The lady was a suffragette, campaigning for women's right to vote, and she devised this suicidal stunt to call public attention to their cause. Eventually English women got the right to vote, but it didn't help this lady. She died several days later from injuries. (The horse and jockey survived without serious damage.)

We doubt even more strongly that willing "cats" would find it possible to grab at bridles or lie down on the racing strip in front of the horses. It just isn't that simple for a spectator to get onto the track. Besides the wire fences and the guards, there will be that almost solid wall of race fans lining both sides. Just their being packed along the rails is enough to block off any sort of demonstration.

Any real interference with the actual running of the race, from inside the track, seems beyond the capabilities of Gregory's fans. Actually the only hint of any such fanatic exercise has been in Gregory's quoted line, and other Negro leaders here have talked only of demonstrations on the outside.

Street marches, for instance, or a slow parade of cars to interfere with Derby traffic. This is the sort of thing they have suggested, and obviously these acts could present problems. But they would be problems only of inconvenience or delay—the Derby would still be run before the standard "more than 100,000" fans.

Before they do anything, however, the Negro leaders should ask themselves one question—"Will it help?"

Will it help create public sympathy for their cause, for instance, because this is the idea behind all such demonstrations. The answer can only be no, it won't. Most Louisvillians can't see any connection between the Derby and civil rights, and they will resent attempts by anybody to interfere with our one day in the sun.

Will it help convince the Board of Aldermen? No. This, like we said in the beginning, will take an act of God. It is beyond the power of mortal man to inject reason, logic and common sense into nine hunks of solid concrete.

To get mad at the Negroes of this community for threatening to stop the Derby is easy, quite easy. It's almost an instinctive reaction.

To understand why they should want to do such a thing isn't easy at all. It requires thought, and when you ask the average man to think you are asking too much. You just can't get him to remember that the Declaration of Independence reads: " We hold these truths to be self-evident—that all men are created equal."

He prefers to believe it reads, "all white men."

He cannot realize that the Negroes are not asking him to give them equal rights, because the rights are not his to give. These are the rights a Negro is born with, and all he wants is for the white man to stop taking them away.

It's sickening here in Louisville to hear white men prattle about property rights and constitutional rights. Even if they were being asked to give up one tiny particle of their precious rights—and they are not—would it be too much to atone for the century of injustice the Negroes have suffered?

For most of them, it is too much. They prefer to cling to this tiny particle, using it as a cover for their true feelings.

To obtain the rights they were born with, but which they have never been permitted to enjoy, the Negroes of Louisville have tried asking. They asked politely, so as not to offend the plantation mentalities in public office. When they were refused, they asked again. They are still asking, and they are still being refused.

They have been patient, they have been polite, and they have gotten nothing except insulting, patronizing refusals. Not a hope or a promise; just a lecture on conduct, a warning not to rebel.

This is why the Negroes march, why they demonstrate, why some of their so-called spokesmen make wild statements. They are still searching for a way to get some small measure of the justice which is theirs by birth, rather than the injustice which that birth has brought upon them. The wrongs they do in this search are but a fraction of the wrongs they have endured. Before you condemn what they are doing, pause and reflect on what has been done to them—then try to remember when you stood up to protest that.

The unrest of the summer of 1967 brought a request from the Ku Klux Klan for a downtown march and a repartee from the *Irish American*.

Not Even for Laughs?
June 17, 1967

This week the Louisville Department of Public Safety rejected a Ku Klux Klan request for a downtown parade Saturday, based on an opinion by City Law Director Eugene H. Alvey.

Well, that's the way it is. There's a pooper in every party. This time it's Alvey.

Doesn't our law director know we're heading for a long hot summer, we've all got worries about the war in Viet Nam, the shaky peace in the Middle East, crab grass, dandelions, all the ills that mortal man is heir to?

These are the times that try men's souls. We all need a little relief, a chance to laugh. Wasn't it Abraham Lincoln who said, in the midst of the terrible Civil War, that if he could not laugh he would die?

Now here we have a bunch of clowns who offer to supply, absolutely free, a great comedy performance, and what does Alvey do? He tells them no.

Why, the kleagle himself said the KKK marchers wouldn't be masked, so they wouldn't be violating that non-existent ordinance. Here the Kleagle was just going along with the popular opinion, because actually those things they wear over their heads are not really masks.

They are form-fitting hoods. The climax of their whole hilarious comedy routine is when the marchers pull them off and you get to see the incredible pointed heads inside. You just can't hardly stop laughing.

All is not yet lost, however. The kleagle says they will still assemble downtown and mingle with the crowds, wearing their bedsheets but not the hoods. If you're looking for some cheap laughs, downtown Louisville will be the spot.

Just how many pointheads will be there the kleagle didn't say. Letters, he said, were sent to members in Kentucky, Indiana, Virginia and Tennessee.

Now if these members can just find somebody to read the letters to them . . .

8

The City Scene

The city of Louisville in 1950, with a population of some 370,000, ranked twenty-fifth in size among American cities, still considerably larger than such other southern centers as Atlanta, Nashville, and Miami. In that mid-century year, public high schools had just been integrated by gender but would not witness racial integration for another six years. The public library system, with the exception of Western Branch, was still closed to African–Americans, as were the vast majority of parks, restaurants, hotels, and theaters.

This "Gateway to the South" or "Falls City," as it styled itself, was still a muscular, industrial center, with its economy driven by the production of such items as whiskey, cigarettes, beer, and of course Louisville Sluggers. No expressways or shopping malls had yet intruded on the landscape. For a regional city, Louisville even then had a lively reputation in the arts, aided immeasurably by its maverick mayor, Charles P. Farnsley (1907-90), whose creativity had led several national magazines to feature His Honor and his city. The Bingham family's *Courier-Journal* was one of America's leading newspapers.

Over the next two decades, the Kentucky metropolis had a lot of growing up to do. Much of the strain and stress of such growth was to be chronicled in the pages of the *Irish American*. (Discussion of local racial issues by the *Irish American* is to be found in Section 7.)

When Mayor Farnsley headed to the Indianapolis 500 and remarked that "horses are sort of obsolete," editor Barry playfully composed a political obituary.

Farnsley Commits Political Suicide

June 2, 1951

It's a good thing Charles P. Farnsley got himself elected mayor for a 4-year term in 1949. At the expiration of his present term in 1953, he will retire from politics and become

Chancellor of the University of Louisville, according to a story published last year by C-J Sports Editor Earl Ruby.

Farnsley had better make Ruby's prediction come true by quitting politics, because he certainly committed political suicide this week. Visiting Indianapolis for the 500-mile Speedway madness, the Louisville Mayor was quoted by the Associated Press as being convinced "horses are sort of obsolete."

That was horrible enough, but then Farnsley had to pile sacrilege upon sacrilege by adding, "Nobody would wait in line several days to get into the Kentucky Derby like they do at the Speedway."

The horror of it all leaves one aghast.

The few renegade Kentuckians who do go to Indianapolis usually have the decency to sneak away from their homes quietly on the morning of Memorial Day, so as not to offend their neighbors. Then, when by some miracle they survive the perils of the amateur racers on U.S. 31 and return that night unscathed, they can just say, "Oh, we went for a little ride," or "Had a nice picnic with my wife's cousins."

Not knowing for sure that they went to the Speedway, the neighbors can't burst out with, "You mean you went to that crazy auto race? You got rocks in your head or something?"

This keeps the neighborhood at peace, a condition which cannot exist when one Kentuckian defies his heritage and goes to an auto race.

But Farnsley, with a callous disregard for the feelings of his fellow-citizens, goes up to Indianapolis openly! He didn't even try to disguise himself by wearing a four-in-hand tie.

That in itself was bad—very bad.

When he added that awful line about "horses are sort of obsolete," he exposed himself to mob violence upon his return, assuming he dares to return.

But then Farnsley went beyond the pale. To mention the Indianapolis madness in the same breath with the great Kentucky Derby is heresy, but Farnsley did it, and rated the Derby second!

There are not words to describe the depths to which this once-popular Mayor has now sunk in the estimation of his constituents. Suffice it to say Charles Peaslee Farnsley is through, washed-up, finished.

He was a good guy when he had it, but he hasn't got it any more. If he ran for dog-catcher no self-respecting dog would vote for him.

("I know why Charley was crazy about that Indianapolis thing" explained a friend. "It was five hundred miles—and all one-way!")

The arrest of two police officers in May 1951 offered the opportunity for the *Irish American* to take on two of its favorite targets: the Police Department and the *Courier-Journal.*

Police Hit New Low

June 2, 1951

To the surprise of no reader of the Kentucky Irish American, two of Louisville's noble 100 per cent-honest civil service police were arrested last week for the lowest crime in the books—they rolled a drunk.

That was a week ago, but there has been no editorial mention yet in the Holier-Than-Thou Courier Journal, the paper which has long contended honest law enforcement can be obtained only through civil service. Any officer who gets his post through political appointment, or by the process of being elected by a majority of his fellow-citizens, automatically becomes suspected by the Courier.

The rumor that a man has bet a dollar on a horse out in the county rouses the C-J to furious activity. Reporters and photographers are hurriedly dispatched to cover this complete breakdown of law and order, and old familiar editorials are trotted out denouncing county officials. We should merge the city and county governments, says the C-J, and put everybody under that ever-lovin' civil service.

If the performance of the Louisville police is a criterion, perhaps merger would be a good idea. Our coppers could teach the county police not to bother with petty graft, but to put collections on a business basis. The Louisville civil service wonders could show their cohorts how to handle traffic arguments—shoot first and argue later—where to get bargains in automobiles (no heaters necessary, they stay hot all the time) and a few other profitable tricks they have picked up through the years.

But rolling drunks—oh, no! How low can they get?

In 1952, former Louisville mayor and eminent citizen Wilson W. Wyatt Sr. served as national campaign director for Democratic presidential candidate Adlai Stevenson. Wyatt's bald pate, resembling Stevenson's, resulted in a modest editorial proposal.

John W.W.W.W. Today

October 4, 1952

Just as the Republicans charged a couple of months ago, the selection of Wilson Wyatt as his personal campaign manager was Stevenson's first mistake. While most of us around here are familiar with our former Mayor's ability and energy, we must admit he is sadly lacking in one vital requisite for the job.

Wyatt hasn't enough hair.

At first glance, this seems odd. The most successful campaign manager of our times was Jim Farley, who had a beautiful head of skin, but his candidate was sufficiently endowed.

Wyatt's man isn't. Governor Stevenson is one of those fellows who can't stop washing his face until he reaches the back of his neck. When he goes into a barber shop, the only thing taken off the top is his hat.

The lack of hair, to the Democratic candidate himself, is a matter of no consequence. But the absence of it on his campaign manager's scalp is fast becoming a major issue.

As you know, the Democratic Party's big problem has been to sell their candidate to the people. Stevenson was comparatively unknown outside of his home state until the convention, and so the idea has been to show him in as many places as possible in the limited time.

But there's been an unexpected stumbling block. From all over the country come reports of well-intentioned audiences bursting into applause at the sight of Wilson Wyatt. The people, not having seen Stevenson in person, start cheering the first bald head they see.

Lowell Thomas spoke of it on his radio program this week. After the crowd had cheered Wyatt at one place, said Mr. Thomas, the people realized their mistake. Slightly embarrassed and confused, they next cheered Vic Sholis (Lowell called him "Vic Shultess"), one of the top brass of WHAS on lend lease to the Stevenson campaign.

The situation obviously is becoming critical. One panicky Democrat said this week he's afraid Ike will win on a split vote—some of the states being counted on for Stevenson may go to Wyatt.

Desperate times call for desperate measures, so this Democrat wants to organize what he calls a "4-W Club."

"Just a minute," a listener said. "I've heard of a 4-H Club, but what's this 4-W business?"

"Simple," said the Democrat. "A Wig for Wilson Wyatt. We buy him a big bushy scalp-muff, see and then everybody will know who he ain't. Let's see, fire-engine red's a good color, you can see it a long way off . . ."

Send your contribution today. The future of democracy may hang by a hair.

When Louisville went on daylight saving time, several nearby rural residents expressed opposition. The *Irish American* was not amused.

Daylight Saving Squawks Start

February 7, 1953

Now comes the happy time for us city people. The announcement has been made that voluntary daylight saving time will be observed again this year, beginning the last of April, and already the appleknockers and the hayshakers have stated squawking.

While daylight saving time itself is quite enjoyable, the real pleasure comes in hearing the rubes scream their thick heads off. As we've pointed out so many times before, what the clock says never means anything to a farmer, who works by the sun. What gets these plow-jockeys wild is the thought that we city slickers can do as we please.

They neglect their hillbilly programs on radio and television taking this valuable time to write letters to the Courier-Journal Point-of-View column, wherein they insist daylight saving time is indecent, immoral, unethical, illegal and a flagrant defiance of the Revealed Word.

To sit and read these letters aloud is a wonderful soothing tonic for city dwellers, particularly those of us who suffer from rage and frustration when we think of our tax money used to guarantee these rubes a fat living, to hold up prices for the things they grow. . . .

Just sit quietly and read their letters. it's music, that's what it is—sweet music.

Editor Barry took a dour moral view of certain New York stage shows playing in the city in the mid 1950s.

Broadway's Best, It Says
September 15, 1956

In order to get some shows here this winter at the Memorial Auditorium, local theater fans are being solicited to buy tickets for five plays in advance. By thus guaranteeing N.Y.'s Council of The Living Theatre "a ready-made audience," the local group backing the plan believes we can secure for Louisville "the brightest season of stage shows this community has experienced in years."

That's fine, but what about the shows?

These are described as "Broadway's best presentations." From a box-office standpoint, this is probably right, but there is often a wide gap between what New York and Louisville audiences regard as entertainment

Four plays are listed, the fifth to be announced later. Already scheduled are "Janus," "Pajama Game," "Cat On A Hot Tin Roof" and "Hatful of Rain."

"Pajama Game" is a musical comedy with two hit songs, "Hey There" and "Hernando's Hideaway." Based on a funny book, it apparently has a lot of laughs and should furnish a pleasant evening.

But the other three are not so easy to rate.

"Janus," for instance, is a comedy based on adultery. It had a fair run on Broadway, opening with the incomparable Margaret Sullivan. One road company will have Joan Bennett, a faded movie actress who's never done much on the legitimate stage, while the local cast will have Imogene Coca, Sid Caesar's homely ex-TV wife. However, despite Boyd Martin's campaign, there are some Louisvillians who never consider adultery justified and seldom think it's funny.

"Cat On A Hot Tin Roof" is like those TV shows you get about every other Sunday night on moral and physical decay in the Deep South, except that this one has heavy overtones of homosexuality. Such stark "realism" may not appeal to people who think an evening at the theatre should be fun.

"Hatful of Rain" shows the agonizing experiences of a narcotics addict.

A year and a half ago many Louisville theatre-goers were dismayed to learn too late what "Tea and Sympathy" was about. Led astray by the innocent title, and uninformed by the drama reviewers of the Courier-Journal and Times, they bought tickets and were in their seats before they could believe their eyes and ears. Some got up and walked out;

others stayed but warned friends who had bought tickets for later nights.

We believe, therefore, that when the local sponsors ask people here to subscribe for the season, they should give them some idea of what the plays will be about.

It is possible that the shows above will play to sell-out audiences at every performance, and that the patrons will be perfectly satisfied with what they see and hear.

Provided, that is, they know what they are buying.

An Ohio River flood in 1964 caught the city off guard, despite its extensive flood protection system. Scuba divers had to be deployed to extricate floodgates from their flooded quarters. Barry could not resist needling City Hall.

Did They Have to Say Flood?

March 21, 1964

Here in Louisville we have another instance of Mayor Cowger's trouble with the Courier-Journal and Times. On Wednesday the mayor sent a memo to all city department heads and their employees saying:

"Henceforth I would appreciate your refraining from giving any information concerning this City Government to Mr. Jack Ayer and Mr. Peter Milius, reporters for The Courier-Journal and the Louisville Times.

"We have determined that these two reporters are incapable of presenting all the true facts to the people concerning the operation of this City Government."

When the reporters asked Mayor Cowger about the memo, he first said, "I don't care to go into it with you," and walked away. When they pressed him, the mayor said, "I don't care about inaccurate stories you write about me, but I do care about inaccurate stories you write about the whole community."

Asked for examples, Mayor Cowger said, "I think if you had read your stories over the last week, you'll find many examples."

Gosh, you can't blame the mayor for getting mad. Those poison penners did write some terrible stuff.

They said we had a flood, which is definitely a scare word. Why couldn't they have described it as excess moisture or a record dew? No need to be alarmists.

The reporters also said the City had trouble closing the gates in the flood wall. Of all the outrageous lies, this is the worst. The record will clearly show that in every case where the City authorities handled the job, the gates were gotten up in time to prevent a single drop of water from flowing back into the river.

In one instance these skilled operators cleverly put the gate on the wrong side, so that the pressure of the water trapped behind the wall wouldn't force it out of position.

True, one of the top officers in the Corps of Engineers did say, "This is the most fouled-up job I've seen in my life—and I've been in the Army," but he was obviously jealous. His men only knew how to put up the gates the right way.

The Times reporters also proved themselves totally unable to understand the subtle nuances of the Mayor's statements. Cowger carefully explained he had fired Works Director Friend Lodge for giving him inaccurate information but that Lodge hadn't lied to him and he had really worked hard and everybody had worked hard and after all he had made a hundred right decisions and just one little old wrong decision on the 10th Street gate that would cost the companies around there only about half a million dollars and the losses were being blown all out of proportion and he was never going to run for office again except maybe for the sheer joy of beating the Courier-Journal and if they didn't stop saying thank you Dr. Strangelove he wouldn't say another word and . . .

"Miss Lennie" McLaughlin (1900-1988) was one of the few women in America of her era to lead a big-city Democratic party organization as "party boss." Her resignation in 1965 brought forth an appreciative farewell.

Wise Decision

December 11, 1965

An era ended in local and state politics this week when Miss Lennie McLaughlin retired as executive secretary of the Jefferson County Democratic Party. She has been a strong voice in the party for forty years.

Chairman Tom Carroll said there would be no replacement for Miss Lennie; just a part-time employee to help with precinct organization.

This is a wise decision, because he could not possibly replace Miss Lennie. There just isn't anybody around who knows as much about running a political organization, or about handling people, or how to get the good government that will keep the party in power.

Miss Lennie was frequently attacked, criticized, denounced. Those who attacked her were either members of the opposition who did it for political effect, or would-be candidates she had scornfully refused to support, or knuckleheads who didn't know what they were talking about. Very few people in either party were subjected to so much criticism that had utterly no basis in fact.

But the men she helped elect—presidents, senators, governors, mayors—all knew Miss Lennie's real quality. And the hundreds and hundreds of "little people," the precinct workers and small job-holders, will miss the one party leader who never failed them when they needed help.

The many citizens of Louisville who do not know of Miss Lennie's many real contributions to better government naturally can't be expected to express any gratitude. The Democrats—and Republicans—who do know have no such excuse.

All the best, Miss Lennie, all the best.

For a brief while in 1967, Kansas City's Charles Finley talked of moving his major league baseball franchise to Louisville. The *Irish American* sniffed a ruse.

Another Flop Coming Up

August 26, 1967

Back in January, 1964, Finley announced he was considering a move to Louisville.

Immediately the natives were in an uproar. Hooray! Louisville's going to be in the big leagues! Our All American Mayor, William O. Cowger, even got together with Governor Breathitt to discuss what they could do to speed Finley's journey from Kansas City to Fairgrounds Stadium.

In all the excitement, ours was the only voice raised in opposition. The Kentucky Irish American wrote: "What Mayor Cowger should have done was to ask Governor Breathitt to declare martial law, then order all available National Guard units here at once. Isn't this the proper procedure when invasion is threatened?

"Instead, the Mayor and the Governor got together to negotiate a surrender, and are now engaged in lending aid and comfort to the enemy . . . At this writing, Finley's Irregulars are planning to move upon our fair city . . .

"What Louisvillians have ever done to deserve such a fate we don't know . . . If we can hold out until the other American League club owners can mount a rescue force . . .

"Otherwise, disaster . . .

"This is madness. If Finley wants to use Louisville to pry better conditions out of Kansas City, that's his affair, but for our people to aid and abet him is inexcusable."

As the embarrassed Mayor and Governor learned later, Finley never had any intention of moving his team to Louisville. He was using us, just as he has used other people and other places.

But nobody else said so in 1964 except this paper.

Incidentally, while we're beating this particular drum, we might as well say right now that Louisville isn't going to be a major league pro basketball town, either. That otherwise splendid monthly "Louisville," published by the Chamber of Commerce, has an article in the August 20 issue titled "We're a Major League Town Now" that begins:

"Dissenters and doubting Thomases to the contrary, Louisville has become the home of a major-league professional basketball team. The Kentucky Colonels of the new American Basketball Association have set up shop in the downtown Convention Center and all phases are 'go' for the club . . . Chamber of Commerce Sports Committee Chairman Louis M. Benn put it succinctly: 'If we want Louisville to be known as a big league town, we've got to support professional sports, and basketball is a natural for this area.' . . ."

Kindly enroll the K.I.A. as the No. 1 dissenter and doubting Thomas. The way we see it, all phases are "no" for this venture. It has two chances for success—slim and none.

Louisville is already a big league town in its own fashion. We have the Derby, the best known race in the world.

We have the U. of L. Cardinals, a major power in college basketball.

We have Frank Beard and Bobby Nichols, two excellent pro golfers and two of the finest walking advertisements any community could possibly have.

It is ridiculous to say that Louisville's big league ranking depends on the willingness of people to support one particular commercial enterprise, especially one with so little to offer.

The Kentucky Derby constituted the special pride not only of the city but of editor Barry as well.

Our Day Is Here

May 2, 1959

This Saturday is Derby Day, when we in Louisville play host to the most colorful, dramatic and exciting sports event of the year.

But the Derby isn't a Louisville race, or a Kentucky race. It's an American institution.

There was a time when this wasn't so. Back some 40 years a man named Sam Riddle, who didn't deserve to own a horse as good as Man o' War, wouldn't send his champion here for the Derby. He lived long enough to realize his mistake, even if he never admitted it.

Now it's unthinkable that the owner of a horse good enough to run in the Derby would refuse to enter his colt. To win the Derby is the dream of every owner, and the big field this week is testimony to the fact that just having a starter is honor enough for most men.

We've got the right race in the right place—the Derby in Kentucky, the storied home of the thoroughbred. The time is right—the first Saturday in May, when the grass is green, the dogwood's in bloom, morning's at seven and all's right with the world.

We've got the right distance—"a mile and a quarter without any water." Ten furlongs, as Ben Jones once said, is too far for the sprinters, too short for the plodders. It's a real test of both speed and stamina, a searching test, a fair test.

It takes a race horse to win the Kentucky Derby. It's been won by champions and by lesser horses—but they were all champions the day they had to be.

All of these things are on the record. They are known to all men who know horses.

To you who live here, who know the Derby, just this: Be proud. Make it a quiet sort of pride, but let it glow enough on the inside to show just a little on the outside.

It isn't necessary to remind you to be a little extra nice to visitors. These people are our guests. While we're showing them our best horses, let's show them our best manners.

(Now they're all in the gate . . . Steady, boy, steady . . . Get his head up there, Arcaro . . . Watch it, Willie . . . THEY'RE OFF!)

Derby pride also meant that the *Irish American* was on the alert to snippy out-of-town sportswriters.

Sticks and Stones Department
May 18, 1963

Two New York sports writers with widely syndicated columns gave our town the usual treatment after the Derby. Here are some excerpts:

Jimmy Cannon: "Louisville is Scranton, Pa., with red eye gravy. It is strictly a brown shoes with blue suit town . . . As the field for the Derby took the track, Churchill Downs resembled an alcoholics anonymous convention that broke training with a three-day bender . . . The track is ruthlessly mercenary. Even the owners of Derby horses must buy their own seats . . . The entire town is engaged in a big hustle . . . Business was off in the mid-town restaurants all week. Tired of getting clipped, a lot of people arrived by plane Saturday morning and went back to the airport immediately after the Derby . . . Louisville's a distillery town. There seems to be a loan company in every office building and many pawn brokers. It's only logical to assume then that Louisville's main products are paupers and lushes. . . . At a dinner party in a restaurant, a girl from one of Kentucky's old families showed me a pistol she carries in her purse to protect herself. 'Who's bothering you?' I asked. 'You never know,' she replied . . "

Red Smith: "Probably it's just as well. If a horse with the sacrilegious name of No Robbery had won, Churchill Downs would surely have been put to the torch by Louisville hotel proprietors, taxi tycoons and restaurateurs maddened by this desecration of everything Louisville hotel proprietors, taxi tycoons and restaurateurs hold dear. With ice cubes at only $1.51 a bucket, did the man say 'dear?'

"Pockets swollen like their victims' heads, the larcenous natives of this teeming clip joint now resume their workaday occupation of pumping bourbon into chocolate candies, comforted by the knowledge that they celebrated the 89th Derby by swindling more suckers more scandalously than ever before . . ."

* * *

We are happy to report that both Messrs. Cannon and Smith have since arrived safely back in New York, that haven of openhearted generosity where every native's hand is outstretched (palm up) to welcome the weary visitor, where nobody drinks to excess, no hotel proprietors ask top prices or taxi drivers charge a whole dollar, and where a girl doesn't need a pistol for protection, particularly in Central Park. (She needs a flamethrower.)

Civic pride did not prevent a realistic look at problems in the city related to the Derby. Nor did it prevent some tongue-in-cheek suggestions.

Safety Rule for Derby Visitors
May 5, 1956

The thousands of visitors coming here this weekend for the Derby ought to be given a little advice. Follow these rules for instance:

1. Don't bring your car here.
2. Don't bring any valuables.
3. Don't come unarmed.

This week the FBI issued its annual bulletin of crime reports. As usual, our fair city of Louisville made a splendid showing. In our class—cities of 300,000 to 400,000 population—we were first in auto thefts, first in robberies, and first in larcenies over $50.

That's pretty good. Only seven classifications of crimes, and we knocked off first money in three.

Didn't do too bad right down the line, either. Only Oakland nosed us out of burglaries, and we were third in assaults and third in murders. In other words, in six of the seven classifications we finished in the money.

Only in larcenies under $50 did we make a poor showing. Dropped all the way down to seventh, which is probably due to the fact that our thieves find the richer hauls so easy they just don't bother with the petty stuff.

Obviously, any Derby visitor bringing his car here is just trying to collect on his theft insurance. The same thing applies for valuables—the No. 1 city in robberies and larcenies over $50 is hardly the safest place to be when you're wearing jewels or carrying cash.

And, inasmuch as we were a bang-up third in assaults and murders, a visitor would be smart to bring along the ol' equalizer.

9

The Passing Show

The *Kentucky Irish American* pursued its journalistic mission with a distinctive style. This might include its not-infrequent slams at those *other* Louisville papers, the *Courier-Journal* and *Louisville Times*. It might mean quotations from famous figures in large boxes on the front page, a humorous year-end review of local events, an annual list of offbeat New Year's resolutions, the occasionally zingy cartoon, or an unconventional offer of Christmas subscriptions.

Especially in the early 1950s, the *Irish American* directed many of its editorial energies against the Bingham press, which had recently (1948) moved its *Courier-Journal* and *Louisville Times* to Sixth and Broadway.

Courier Journal Again Attacks Ireland
August 26, 1950

The late Judge Bingham, who got an ambassadorship to England because of his great love of that country—and a $50,000 contribution to Roosevelt's campaign fund—would be proud to know the paper he bought some 33 years ago is still carrying on for the deah old Empah! The C-J slogan is still "Hooray for the British! Down with the dirty Irish!"

Thursday of this week one C-J editorial writer, inspired by a steaming cup of tea and munching daintily on a crumpet, denounced Irish leaders as international blackmailers because they still oppose partition.

"The people of Eire," said the C-J, "lack only the privilege of forcing their will on the Protestant majority in Ulster . . . The people of Ulster voted three to one against joining Eire in February, 1949, in a parliamentary election that brought out 90 percent of the vote. The cause of liberty would certainly be insulted if the great majority of Ulsterites were forced to give up their freedom to join a state they detest. Eire's insistent demand for the six counties has two enormous defects: it is impossible of achievement, and it is wrong in principle."

Wrong in principle? Was it right in principle for the English Parliament to erect this political minority into a satellite statelet 30 years ago, without consulting the wishes even of its own inhabitants? What did the C-J say then?

"The February, 1949, election," wrote the Rev. Thomas L. Coonan, Associate Professor of History at St. Louis University, "was about as free as an election in Russia . . . The Six County imposture is one of those extraordinary phenomena which have neither real nor apparent justification on political, economic, cultural or geographic grounds . . . There is not and never was a religious problem in Ireland except the one created by English misrule in the sixteenth and seventeenth centuries. There is not and never was a political problem precluding the unity of Ireland. In the eighteenth century the Presbyterians were the Sinn Feiners . . . Russia exults at the existence of such Western political crimes as the partition of Ireland."

It's too much, though, to expect the British-loving Courier-Journal to be fair and impartial in any question involving England. Every time the band plays "America," the C-J editorial staff stands up and sings "God Save The King."

In the very early 1950s, the *Irish American* decided that the *Courier-Journal* had gone soft on local gambling corruption.

Practices Against Own Preaching

January 27, 1951

Now that you consider it, it's hard to understand how eating the crow Sheriff Bax served up should give the C-J boys upset stomachs. After all the stuff they've swallowed for years, they should have the digestion of a billygoat.

The Courier-Journal supports birth control. It willingly

publishes ads for strip-tease shows. Its movie critic invariably approves all foreign movies, based on sex, as "art."

It sends its reporters out like bloodhounds to track down every rumor of corruption in office. Political office, that is. Just this past week, on the flimsiest sort of evidence, the C-J practiced the smear technique it professes to abhor by putting the name of Emerson "Doc" Beauchamp in a Page One headline, linking the commissioner of rural highways with the alleged $6,000 bribe. Only a small percentage of readers followed the story far enough down to discover that two witnesses had told conflicting stories, neither of which could be proved, regrading Mr. Beauchamp's presence when someone else is supposed to have received the money. Still the C-J smeared him just the same.

But the Courier won't touch the Louisville Police Department. Our police, high and low, in and out of uniform, have openly collected toll from Louisville gamblers for years and years, but not ONE SINGLE TIME have the C-J's bloodhound reporters come up with a story.

In fact, the Courier-Journal endorses this taking of bribes. A few months ago, on the page facing its weaseling editorials, a C-J writer quoted an unnamed police official as saying he didn't blame our poor underpaid police for "taking a little on the side."

There wasn't a peep out of the ivory heads in the editorial ivory tower, so apparently they didn't blame our poor, underpaid police either. Can you imagine the outbursts if a political office-holder, say Sheriff Bax, had openly stated his deputies were underpaid and he wouldn't blame them for picking up a little extra?

The explosion at Sixth and Broadway would make Bikini sound like a popcorn bag.

Although hard-pressed for space, the C-J last week found plenty of room to reprint in full an article attacking the Irish. Written by a renegade named Peter Kavanagh, it had appeared originally in the American Mercury, whose permission to reprint the Courier eagerly sought.

Anything against the Irish, or praising the British, is grist for the C-J mill. While they were delighted to run the whole piece, they were doubtless overjoyed at the opportunity to print this line:

"The Irishman needs opposition to feed his emotional temperament, and if he does not get sufficient opposition he becomes flabby and crooked, like Irish-American politicians . . ."

Louisville's history has a long list of Irish-American politicians—Matt O'Doherty, Frank Dugan, John and Jim Whallen, Frank McGrath, John O'Brien, John J. Barry, Mike Brennan, Pat Welsh—these names are readily recalled.

Would the Courier care to say any one of the above was flabby and crooked?

Ever since Judge Bingham bought the paper with his hard-earned money, the C-J's policy has been rabidly pro-British. Back around 1920, when British military police staged a reign of terror in Ireland, shooting, killing, executing, breaking into private homes and churches, arresting priests, the C-J editorials were singing "God Save the King."

In 1933 the Judge secured the precious privilege of close association with his beloved British by paying $50,000 more of his hard-earned money into the Democratic campaign fund, getting in return the appointment as ambassador to the Court of St. James.

Sure the money was hard-earned! Is there any harder way of earning it?

According to the *Irish American*, the *Courier-Journal* had difficulty being positive about any Kentucky governor.

The Narrow Groove of Choice

February 10, 1951

The C-J didn't like the way Governor Clements did things. Its editors disagreed strongly with Governor Willis. They weren't satisfied with Governor Johnson, or with Governor

Chandler. They didn't like Governor Laffoon, or Governor Sampson, or Governor Fields.

It's too bad the Courier wasn't being printed when this state got started. We could have found out what was wrong with Isaac Shelby.

* * *

A few heretics have been heard to say the Courier is wrong, but this isn't possible. In the depths of that mausoleum at Sixth and Broadway, that eight-million-dollar white elephant, is the fount of all wisdom. Gathered in conference, the editorial brains can swiftly solve any problem that ever baffled the minds of ordinary men.

We are indeed a privileged people, here in this area, to be the recipients of this boundless knowledge.

Citizens in other communities are not so fortunate. They have to read two newspapers, sometimes more, in their search for truth. When the two disagree, as often happens, the poor citizens are forced to do their own thinking.

This can be dangerous. Let us be thankful that public opinion in Kentuckiana is being properly molded, by the ever-loving Courier, in the narrow groove of its choice.

The paper must accept responsibility, of course, for all the moldy old public opinions you run into these days.

New Year's Resolutions for 1960

January 2, 1960

Now's the time for our annual invaluable advice on developing your will power. A lot of you, unfortunately, have stopped making New Year's resolutions because you have so much trouble keeping them.

"It's no use," you say. "I just haven't got the will power. If I make any resolutions I'll break 'em sure, and then I'll feel more miserable. It's really better if I don't even try."

Nonsense. Follow the system we give and come January 1, 1961, you can look back on a year of solid achievement.

The idea is to make resolutions you can keep. Just as a strong rope is built up of single strands, so can you develop a will of iron by weaving together these slender reeds.

Here are a few suggestions:

1. I will not say to strange truck drivers, "Climb down outa that cab, you big monkey, and we'll see who's got the right of way!"

2. I will not plan a winter vacation in Cuba.

3. I will not offer to test a radical new development in parachutes.

4. I will not have my wife worrying over where I got the money by surprising her with a mink coat.

5. I will cut down drastically the number of mornings I begin the day with an ice cold shower and a brisk run around the block before breakfast, realizing that this makes my less athletic neighbors insanely jealous.

6. I will not cheat any more on my tax returns. (Any more than I did last year.)

7. I will not say to my children, "Now, when I was your age . . ." because I know they don't believe I ever was.

8. I will not trade a headache for an upset stomach.

9. I will not walk into the boss's office and say, "You may own this business, but you'd fold in a week if I ever left you on your own."

10. I will not bet money (c) on races (a, g, wb) in 1960. (The "c" stands for Confederate, the "a" for armadillo, the "g" for goat, the "wb" for water buffalo.)

Naturally you can add some of your own. Just give the matter a little thought, as little as possible, and you can face the next 52 weeks clear-eyed and unafraid.

A *Catholic Digest* article of October 1961 resulted in a national deluge of requests for subscriptions. The Barry brothers, wanting to be sure new readers grasped their unique style, sent out the following form letter:

October 1, 1961

We appreciate your inquiry regarding this paper.

The price of a year's subscription is $5. We cannot accept subscriptions for less than a year, nor do we make refunds to irate subscribers who wish to cancel when they discover their knotheaded opinions do not agree with our knotheaded opinions.

It may save both of us time and trouble if you know, before you subscribe, some of our views. For instance, we despised Joe McCarthy when he was alive and we hate McCarthyism now.

We agree wholeheartedly with Indiana Governor Matthew Welsh's description of the John Birch Society—"howling jackals of suspicion who talk big and think small, who accuse of treason Americans with whom they disagree and who slander their neighbors with cowardly whispers of disloyalty."

We think Father Ginder, who writes in Our Sunday Visitor, is an incurable knucklehead.

On a variety of other subjects, we're like the old fellow who said, "Well, I haven't made up my mind about that, but when I do I'm going to be bitter, mighty bitter!"

Now that you have some ideas, you may do as you please. It's your money.

It's also our paper.

Mike and Joe Barry

KENTUCKY IRISH AMERICAN
319 W. Liberty
Louisville 2, Ky.

A Warm, Personal Message From the Staff About Christmas Gift Subscriptions

November 20, 1965

In response to unpopular demand, we have decided to accept a limited number of Christmas gift subscriptions. (That's right, unpopular. Do people who demand payment of bills win any popularity contests with you?)

The number we accept will be limited by the amount of money you send in. For subscriptions outside of Louisville, send in a $5 bill and we'll send the paper. For one in Louisville, send in a $3 bill and we'll send a Treasury agent around to your house to ask questions. (Has anybody got three 3's for a 9?)

If you prefer to send checks, please make these payable to the Kentucky Irish American. It does not—repeat not—expedite matters when you send us checks already made out to Churchill Downs, Latonia or Master Clocker's Secret Code Guaranteed Daily Special.

A year of reading makes a splendid gift. If you care enough to send the very best, we can suggest the Atlantic Monthly, Saturday Review, American Heritage and so on. (Also there are stimulating articles in Playboy.)

On the other hand, let's say you're budget-conscious. (This is much more charitable than saying you're tight, stingy or cheap.) In this case, $3 or $5 will fit your pocketbook, your money will fit our most pressing need, and 52 issues of this paper will give anybody fits.

In order to meet our regular publication date, we have arranged this year to have Christmas on December 25, and to have December 25 a Saturday. This will enable us to begin all gift subscriptions with the issue of that week, which will be put in the mail the night of December 23, avoiding the mail-early rush and assuring delivery on December 24.

It is suggested you send in your orders as soon as possible to us at 319 West Liberty, because this offer may be withdrawn at any time. Any time we have that Real Good Day at the track—and remember Latonia runs through December 18.

And remember, it's not the gift, it's the money. If we don't get your money, nobody will get your gift.

The customary handsomely engraved gift card, bearing a handsomely engraved 4-cent stamp, will be sent if you request. If you wish to remain anonymous, just say so. We don't mind at all doing business with cowards, just so they come up with the money.

And a hearty ho-ho-ho to you, too.

In the Christmas season, Barry relished publishing this holiday anecdote with a moral message.

The Monk Who Didn't Sing
December 22, 1956

A Christmas Story

There was once a group of medieval monks who annually prepared a program of Christmas music with great care. One of their number, who sang fervently a little off key, was a source of embarrassment to them. He so loved to participate in the chants that they hesitated to ask him to keep silent. After a few years, however, their pride in the artistic effect of their service was so great that he was requested not to sing.

Christmas came and went. Without the old monk, the music had been absolutely perfect.

However, God said to the angels, "I missed something this year. There used to be an old monk in a certain abbey on earth who sang the most exquisite service. But this Christmas he didn't sing at all."

"But Lord," said one of the angels, "all the other monks sang the service as usual."

"Indeed!" answered the Lord. "I have never heard the others. His was the only voice that ever reached my throne."

Every now and again, editor Barry revealed a domestic touch with vignettes about family life.

A Fable

September 7, 1968

Once upon a time there was a family with half a dozen children of school age. On the first morning of school the mother got up at 6:30 to get them all ready.

When she walked into the kitchen, she was surprised to find her oldest daughter washing dishes.

"What are you doing?" said the mother.

"I'm washing the breakfast dishes," the oldest daughter replied. "I didn't want to leave them for you to do."

"You mean you've already eaten?" said the mother. "What about the others?"

"We've all had breakfast," said the oldest daughter. "I told them all to be real quiet and not wake you up. You need your rest."

"My goodness," the mother said, "that's certainly thoughtful of you. Now I guess I'd better go get the little ones dressed."

"Oh no you don't," said the oldest daughter. "Gwendolyn is taking care of the little ones. You just sit yourself right down here and drink this nice fresh coffee I just made."

As the mother sat down, Gwendolyn brought the little ones out to the kitchen. "Here they are, mother dear," she said, "all ready for inspection."

"Why, they all look fine," the mother said. "And each one has on just the right clothes!"

"Look!" said one of the little children. "It's starting to rain!"

"Never fear," Gwendolyn said. "I've got all your rubbers and raincoats ready on the porch."

"It's a shame you have to go to school on a rainy day," the mother said. "It's ever so much fun when we're all cooped up together here in the house."

"I know, Mother," the oldest said, "but I for one can't wait to go back. Our new teacher is the strictest in the history of the school—all business and no fooling around. I'm really glad—now there won't be the slightest excuse for my not getting good marks."

"Same with me," Gwendolyn said. "The teacher I've got this year just piles on the homework, so I won't be hanging on the telephone all night or wasting time on those silly television programs."

"Let's hurry," one of the little ones said. "It isn't hardly raining at all, and if we go now we won't have to splash through any puddles."

So the children all went off to school happy and smiling, and the mother relaxed over coffee and the morning paper.

In its last year of publication, the *Irish American* began to place quotations of sages in large boxes on its front page. Placed so prominently, they reveal the editor's own concerns as the paper neared its demise.

Conviction and Intensity
December 16, 1967

The best lack all conviction while the worst are full of passionate intensity.

—Yeats

Happiness
December 30, 1967

The time to be happy is now.
The place to be happy is here.
The way to be happy is to make others happy.
—Robert Ingersoll

Patriotism
January 6, 1968

It is the noisy, brash, moronic "patriot," and not the thoughtful critic, who is the dangerous citizen.

—Elmer Davis

Formula for Failure
January 13, 1968

I cannot give you the formula for success, but I can give you the formula for failure: Try to please everybody.

—Herbert Bayard Swope

Greatness of Civic Spirit
April 6, 1968

Those whom Nature has endowed with the capacity for administering public affairs should put aside all hesitation, enter the race for public office, and take a hand in directing the government; for in no other way can a government be administered or greatness of spirit be made manifest.

—Cicero

Prejudice
June 8, 1968

Prejudice is the number one mental health problem in America. It costs more and damages more children, both those who are taught it and those who are victims of it, than any other form of mental illness.

—Sen. Fred R. Harris
(Alarms and Hopes: A Personal Journal)

Happiness
July 20, 1968

Happiness lies in our destiny like a cloudless sky before the storms of tomorrow destroy the dreams of yesterday and last week.

—Linus

Reformers
August 31, 1968

The world's best reformers are those who begin on themselves.
—Shaw

Scandal and Truth
November 23, 1968

If a scandal come out of the truth, it is better that the scandal come than that the truth be concealed.
—St. Jerome

Human Nature
November 30, 1968

Human nature will not change. In any future great national trial, compared with the men of this, we shall have as weak and as strong, as silly and as wise, as bad and as good.
—Lincoln (1864)

10

The Sporting Life

Reporting on sports in the *Kentucky Irish American* could be described in many ways: conversational, spunky, frisky. It could at times be snippy or critical. It was always distinctive and lively. Although Joe Barry usually covered bowling, editor Mike took on the hoop, the diamond, the gridiron, the ring, and, of course, the turf.

Mike Barry, according to sports historian Jim Bolus, had seen every Kentucky Derby since 1922—World War II years excepted— and was the "Dean of Derby writers." Even from the Pacific war zone, though, he commented on the race through the "Brothers In Arms" column. In the 1980s, when Barry often attended Sunday mass at the chapel at Louisville's Bellarmine College, he was generally given a short time after the liturgy on "Derby Sunday" to explain to the congregation what had happened to his Derby choice.

Though the focus of this anthology has been the political writing of Barry and the *Irish American*, it seemed only fitting to conclude with a short sampler of sports pieces. Avid readers of the *Irish American* almost invariably turned from its front page politics to its back page sports. Here is a sampling of what they read.

The racing turf was sportsman Barry's special domain. Here, in the spring of 1948, he reported on the Derby victory of Calumet Farm's eventual Triple Crown winner, Citation.

Old, Old Story

May 8, 1948

Good old Count Fleet! If it hadn't been for this long-shot (2.80) winner I stabbed in 1943, my Derby record would now be 15 losers in 15 years. As it is, I've only had 14 out of 15.

You've got to admit I'm getting better, too. Last year my Phalanx missed only by a head, and last Saturday Coaltown was nosed out by a mere 3½ lengths. Some people are saying the result would have been different if Jockey Pierson had urged Coaltown a little more vigorously.

I must agree with these people. Had Pierson really booted the colt, I don't think Citation would have beaten him by more than 3½ lengths.

* * *

Oh well, it was just another demonstration of my uncanny ability to pick the loser on a 50-50 proposition. Everybody knew the race was between the Calumet pair—a guy could have tossed a coin and had a 50% chance of being right.

Not me. I don't go in for such slipshod handicapping. I sit down and figure these things out scientifically. Not only did I name Coaltown and Citation one-two, but I predicted the order of finish for the other four starters.

In case you haven't checked, I missed on all six.

It wasn't easy to do, either.

* * *

Seriously, I thought it was one of the finest Derbies in years. There'll be many a racing day before we see the likes of these two again, particularly in the same race. The gal or guy who didn't thrill to the sight of those two champions just isn't a lover of the sport.

I wrote a month ago that if you just wanted to win a bet, you could always do that on a thousand-dollar plater, but seldom in your life would you see a really great racehorse. Saturday you surely saw one, and maybe two. We'll know more about the enduring brilliance of Coaltown after he runs a few more races.

Citation—well, he's everything they say, and more. Incidentally, did you know he's three-fourths British? His grandsire was the imported Bull Dog, and his dam the imported mare Hydroplane II.

In looking into the world of college sports, editor Barry could also at times cast a hard glance at other issues in American civic life.

Racial Fair Play

January 14, 1950

There are now Negro students at Notre Dame. . . . An interesting article in the February issue of *Ebony* Magazine gives the details. "Once Notre Dame was consistently under fire of the Negro press for consistently refusing admission to Negro students," said *Ebony*, "but today men of the Blue and Gold eat, sleep, study, pray and play together without regard for color."

"Cracking of the one-time lily-white policy at Notre Dame came as a result of two pressures: one, insistence by liberal Catholics on admission of Negroes; two, wartime educational programs in which the Navy Department refused to kowtow to long-standing color bans . . .

"Despite the long tradition against admission of Negroes at Notre Dame, the color barriers fell by the wayside easily and smoothly at the school . . . Negroes fresh on the campus were amazed by the total lack of prejudice . . ."

Of course. The ban could have been lifted years ago with the same result, and it should never have been there in the first place.

It would have been far better, though, if Notre Dame had arrived at this decision on her own without being pushed into it by the Navy. No Catholic or Catholic institution should have to be shown the folly of prejudice.

Barry could also become enthusiastic when he spoke of the Hialeah course near Miami.

Oh, Happy Day

January 15, 1951

The patience of my nine readers passeth all understanding. Here I've been cluttering up this valuable space for months with junk about football and basketball, instead of my usual piercing comments on racing, but have they complained?

No, they haven't. Their pockets are probably jammed full of coarse notes by this time, while they wander about in a daze wondering what's happening, but they don't squawk. I'll bet I could neglect 'em until they ran out of boxes to keep their money in, and there'd be nary a beef, but I'm not going to.

Without wasting another week I'm going to start relieving that pressure. It's high time, what with Hialeah opening next Wednesday, that I began to slip the faithful a few goodies.

* * *

I know Hialeah's opening date pretty well, because it happens to be my wedding anniversary. How could a fellow forget a day like that?

My wife hasn't forgotten it—that I know. Just the other evening she was telling some friends about how, when we were leaving the church, I told the driver to go to the Brown Hotel.

"The Brown?" she said. "We're having our wedding breakfast at the Puritan!"

"I know, my love," I said, "but I just want to pick up a Form."

I regret to say that started our very first argument, but we haven't had another one since.

We're still on that first one.

* * *

I remember, too, how I wanted to go to Florida on our honeymoon and the dear girl wanted to go to New York, so we compromised and went to New York.

"It's so expensive up there," I'd say.

"Florida's a bargain," she'd say. "I know it's warm down there, but can we live outdoors?"

"But Hialeah will be running," I'd say. "I'll win our expenses and plenty to boot."

"No," she'd say, "nothing doing. I know girls have walked home from dates before, but I don't want to be the first bride who had to walk home from her honeymoon."

So we went to New York. Never underestimate the power of a woman, I always say.

While Churchill Downs held a special place in the heart of native Louisvillian Barry, he could wax eloquent, even poetic, when Keeneland opened in Lexington every spring. With Victorian poet Robert Browning's "Home Thoughts, From Abroad" in the wings, Barry intoned as follows:

Bluegrass Browning

April 7, 1951

Oh, to be at Keeneland
Now that April's there,
And see your winter's hard-earned dough
Vanish into air!
Where the cold-dope choice and the stable tip
Both run a long mile and lose by a lip,
Where the eaglebird sings on the orchard bough,
At Keeneland—now!

* * *

Next Thursday, you know, is opening day at this beautiful track on the Versailles Pike, and you can be surrounded by beautiful women while you watch those beautiful horses win at beautiful prices.

How anybody can be miserable in the midst of all this loveliness is pretty difficult, but I always manage to do it. Like in anything else, you've got to have confidence to beat the races. At most tracks I've got it, but not at Keeneland. I'm licked when I get there—I know it and they know it.

Those hardboots just sit by the front gate and drool when they see us Louisvillians walk in. You can see 'em nudge each other and say, "Well, here come the chumps to build up the prices. Let's get to bettin'."

* * *

They are so right. I devote my years of handicapping experience to a close study of the Form, calculate the shifting odds on the tote board with lightning rapidity, set it in on something that looks good enough to eat, then stand there and watch him plod home a tired tenth.

That's bad enough, but immediately I seem to be surrounded by laughing Lexingtonians, slapping each other on the back and saying, "Cal told me that mare of his was sharp!" or "I caught her in thirty-five and two on the farm last week!"

The next race I ease up close to these natives and try to pick up something, but all I hear are vague references to "Joe's little colt," "that big-kneed mare the old man worked Friday morning," "the bay from over near my place" and things like that.

Never a name do I hear. Not being a member of the clan, I don't know Joe's colt from Adam's ox. All I know is I'm not in the know, and these guys are.

Oh well, it's a nice drive up there, and the food in the restaurant is delicious.

I wish I could afford it.

When Barry's daughter Jane was about to enter school, he reflected on her precocious insights on the subject of betting.

Little Silver Book

August 7, 1952

My oldest daughter starts to school next month, but the kid will have to make it on her own. No more private lessons at home for little Jane.

About a week ago I suggested to the commanding officer at our headquarters that a little pre-school instruction might help Jane get started. The suggestion was received with suspicion, just as all my suggestions are, but finally the C.O. said I could give it a try.

"This I've got to see," she said.

"But my dear!" I said. "Janey won't be able to concentrate with both of us in the room. You just leave it to her dear old daddy."

It took a lot of fast talking, but I eventually got a reluctant agreement.

The little girl and I started our private lessons, and everything was going along fine until she said the wrong thing at the supper table.

"Weather man said we might have some showers," I said.

"He's been saying that for a week," said my wife. "I'll bet it doesn't rain a drop."

"The more you bet," said Jane, "the more you get."

My wife gave her a startled look. "What did you say?"

"She said we might get some rain," I cut in.

"No, she didn't," said my wife. "Janey, what did you say?"

"Get a hunch and bet a bunch," said Jane. "Isn't that right, daddy?"

"Yes, Janey, that's right," I said. "Now get busy there and eat your supper. You know you won't grow up to be big and strong like daddy unless you eat . . ."

"Wait a minute," cut in the C.O. "I want to know a little more about this. What's all this about bets and hunches and things?"

"That's what daddy taught me," said Jane. "I'm supposed to say that to the other children."

"Oh," she said, "You are, are you? And what other nice things did dear old daddy tell you to say?"

"If you wanna get something," said Jane, "you've gotta bet something."

"Remarkable," said my wife. "What else?"

"I can't think of any more," said Jane.

"Well," she said, "that's enough, I can see he's done quite a job—I'll have to give him credit."

"Oh, no, mother!" said Jane. "You mustn't!"

"Mustn't what?" said my wife.

"You mustn't give anybody credit," said Jane. "Daddy said positively no markers."

"That's all, daughter," she said. "You can run out and play now. I want to have a short talk with dear old daddy."

"Some other time, dear." I said. "I just remembered I've gotta fix that Christmas tree stand—before we know it it'll be Christmas and we'll be rushing around and . . ."

"We'll risk it," she said. "First I've got to know more about my daughter's studies at your little college of fantastic knowledge. What in the world have you been teaching her, bookmaking?"

"I might have known you'd take this attitude," I said. "Just a little instruction in self-defense."

"What's self-defense got to do with it?"

"If she's bookin'," I said, "she won't be bettin'. The world is made up of two classes, layers and players, and I just wanna see that she gets on the right side."

She looked at me. "And you're the guy said Piersall was crazy!"

"Crazy like a fox," I said. "Here, lemme show you this clipping. Read this."

She read the clipping from a New York paper, about how a 19-year-old youth was arrested for running a baseball book at Public School No. 42. The youth was arrested after one of the school kid's parents heard a couple of youngsters boasting, "Boy, we sure hit George today!"

The father questioned the kids and discovered they'd been betting nickels and dimes that they could pick three baseball players who together would get six hits, for which George paid off 10 to 1.

George told police he won 60 per cent of the bets because the "kids played their favorite players, not just good hitters."

Public School 42, around which he operated, consists of grades one through six.

"Why, that's perfectly outrageous!" she said. "I've never heard of anything so terrible!"

"The guy was makin' eight bucks a day on the book," I said. "What's terrible about that?"

She gave me the look.

"Of course I wouldn't expect Janey to do that well right

away," I said, "not with those kids in the first grade, but even a buck a day wouldn't be bad."

"I've got a better idea," she said. "I've just thought of a place where you can run a book yourself."

"Oh, boy!" I said. "Where's that?"

"If you can get a reservation," she said. "I heard they're pretty crowded. Wait till I phone and see . . . Operator, will you get me Highland 7721?"

She talked on the phone a minute and then came away. "They're full up now, but they've promised to save the first vacancy."

I walked around feeling swell for a couple of days until I suddenly got suspicious and looked up Highland 7721.

Then I didn't feel so good. It's Our Lady of Peace Hospital.

In 1955, the Brooklyn Dodgers at last bested the Yankees in World Series play. Dodgers fan Barry was eager to comment.

Goodbye, Mr. Chips

October 8, 1955

I am surprised as anybody over the World Series. Never did I dream that the Yankees, with all their stinking luck, could extend Brooklyn to the limit of seven games. When I picked the Dodgers in four straight, I thought Genius Stengel might just possibly squeeze out one win, but no more.

Three games the Yankees won! Just goes to show you—never underestimate the power of ignorance and luck, even when up against superior science and skill.

Last week, in this space I passed along to you the weird brain waves of a local Yankee follower, Phil Zimmerman, better known as Mr. Chips.

I wanted to bring you this week his afterthoughts on the series, but there has been some delay. The Coast Guard can't find the body.

Mr. Chips was last seen headed for the Clark Bridge with an anvil tied around his neck, and while I hate to think . . .

Me, I took the whole thing very calmly. Any story you may get from my wife or daughters is a wild exaggeration—you know women can never get anything straight.

This is the way it happened. I rushed home Saturday, and while I was struggling to carry the groceries inside I called out "What's the score?"

My daughter Jane—she's the intellectual one—looked up from her comic book and said, "What score?"

"The Yankees and Brooklyn!" I said.

"Oh," said Jane, "we're leading the Dodgers 38 to 14."

I dropped the groceries. "YOU'RE leading the Dodgers! My own flesh and blood a Yankee rooter! A viper in my bosom! And that score—who's pitching now, Dazzy Vance?"

My wife called from the front room. "Please be quiet—I can't hear the announcer!"

I ran in there and she was calmly watching the game, "How can you stand it?" I yelled. "It's a massacre! And our own daughter's rooting for the Yankees!"

"Quiet!" she said. "C'mon, Carl, don't let 'em dig in on you. Stick it in his ear!"

Mike Barry was a slow convert to the pugilistic power of the "Louisville Lip," Muhammad Ali (né Cassius Clay)—even after the Champ's 1964 bout with Sonny Liston.

Float Like a Butterfly

February 29, 1964

I thought the guy in the Coast Guard boat could have been a little more polite. After all, I'm one of the taxpayers who pay his salary.

"Listen, buddy," he said, "pullin' guys like you outa the

water's our job, but you jump offa that bridge one more time we're gonna let you drown."

He really didn't have to worry. After three jumps I was just too pooped to climb up there again.

Pooped is the word that tells the story. After six rounds of chasing Cassius and punching big holes in the air, Liston was just too tired to try any more.

Had he kept on going, I'm convinced Liston would have lost by a KO instead of a TKO. Not that Clay would have knocked him unconscious, but Sonny would have been so completely exhausted the slightest push would have put him down—and he couldn't have gotten up.

The guys who said Clay was too fast and Liston too slow were absolutely right. Sonny hasn't hit him yet.

Now it is Clay who will draw the crowds. Before, they came to see him as a curiosity. Next time they'll respect him as a fighter of ability.

Naturally there's a limit to the amount of crow one man can eat. Therefore I'll have to decline another heaping dish when it gets to the point I have to admit Clay is a fighter of ability.

I'm not going to say that, because I don't believe it. Clay is still the same guy who was life-and-death to get a disputed decision over Doug Jones, the same fellow who was floored by Henry Cooper.

Televised football on Sunday afternoon has convulsed many an American living room. Barry reported on this phenomenon in a first-person narrative.

Sunday Serenade

January 9, 1965

Early last Sunday afternoon, while my wife was talking on the phone in another room, there was an outburst of noise in the living room—loud wails, moans, cries of anguish. My wife calmly went on with the conversation.

"My goodness!" said the lady on the other end of the line. "What's happening at your house?"

"Nothing." said my wife. "Just two o'clock."

"Two o'clock?" said the lady. "It's two o'clock over here too, but all is calm, all is peaceful."

"It wouldn't be," my wife said, "if you had a husband who was a nut on pro football and some kids who like to watch Tarzan movies. Those jungle pictures start at one o'clock and at two Mike changes channels to watch his game. Then the kids start screaming."

"Doesn't it bother you?" asked the lady.

"It did at first," my wife said, "but this has been going on every Sunday since the pro football season started last September. Now I can get my nerves back to normal by Wednesday or Thursday."

The two went on talking another twenty or thirty minutes, just getting warmed up, when suddenly there was another outburst from the living room, this one louder and more bloodchilling than the first. My wife dropped the phone and rushed in.

A few minutes later she walked back to the phone. "Sorry," she told the lady, "but that wasn't on the schedule. I was afraid something was happening to the children."

"Are they all right?" the lady asked.

"They're fine," my wife said. "They're all playing outside. Mike's in there all by himself."

"You mean he made that terrible noise?" the lady asked. "What in the world happened."

"Well," my wife said, "I'll tell you exactly what he told me. He said the Packers blitzed their backers and got bombed. Does that make any sense to you?"

The lady said it didn't. "Not to me, either," said my wife, "but when I asked him what it was he started moaning about a safety dog. I thought for the sake of the children I'd better leave before I started talking like that."

"You poor dear," the lady said. "Just do the best you can and I'll try to come see you on visiting day."

Barry was not a particularly strong fan of Adolph Rupp, the legendary University of Kentucky basketball coach from 1930 to 1972.

Three Little Words

March 26, 1966

Those who watched the NCAA final last Saturday night just couldn't believe their eyes. How could the greatest college basketball team in history lose?

To get an explanation, they asked Adolph Rupp. The old Character Builder gave three answers!

1. His team choked.
2. His team played stupid.
3. His team got robbed by the officials.

Naturally, Rupp didn't give all three of these explanations at the same time. He switched them around to fit his audience.

The "choke" explanation was given to sports writers after the game. Rupp said, "I think the pressure got to the boys . . . If you're going to let pressure get to you, you might as well go home before the game.

The "stupid" explanation went to radio broadcaster Claude Sullivan, who in the post-game interview asked Rupp if he didn't consider Bobby Joe Hill's two steals to be a turning point. "The last thing I told the boys before they left the dressing room," Rupp said, "was to watch out for that. You can't dribble the ball with your head down."

Then, after a day or two to think it over, Rupp produced the "we was robbed" alibi in the proper setting. He appeared before the Lexington Quarterback Club and told them what they wanted to hear. "You give us 34 free throws and give the Boston Celtics 13 and we'll give them a good run for it."

Well, there you are. If any of you care to argue with this

Trew Blew Sportsman, go right ahead. Just deal me out—I know when I'm overmatched.

All I'll say is what I've said all year,—the 1965-66 season was a lean year for basketball. There were a lot of pretty good teams, but not really one solid, first-class ball club to compare with those of the past half-dozen years. Not one.

Index

Abbreviations

CJ<: *Courier-Journal and Louisville Times*; JB: John J. Barry; *KIA*: *Kentucky Irish American*; MB: Mike Barry

www.ingramcontent.com/pod-product-compliance
Lightning Source LLC
Chambersburg PA
CBHW020941310726
48980CB00001B/11

* 9 7 8 0 8 1 3 1 1 8 9 8 7 *